SEVERN TUNNEL TO NEWPORT

C O
B43428

THE SOUTH WALES MAIN LINE
PART TWO

SEVERN TUNNEL TO NEWPORT

BY JOHN HODGE

Featuring the photographs of John Hodge and others

DEDICATION

I dedicate this book to the late Richard Manley, my Uncle Dick, who worked on the railway at Newport, first as a Checker at Newport Goods and then, during the 1950s and 60s, as a Signalman at East Mendalgief Box, outside Pill Shed. I used to visit him there and go in search of the last Newport & Alexandra Docks & Railways Nos. 666 and 667, and watch the iron ore for Ebbw Vale come off South Quay up to Mendalgief Bank where the 92s would take over.

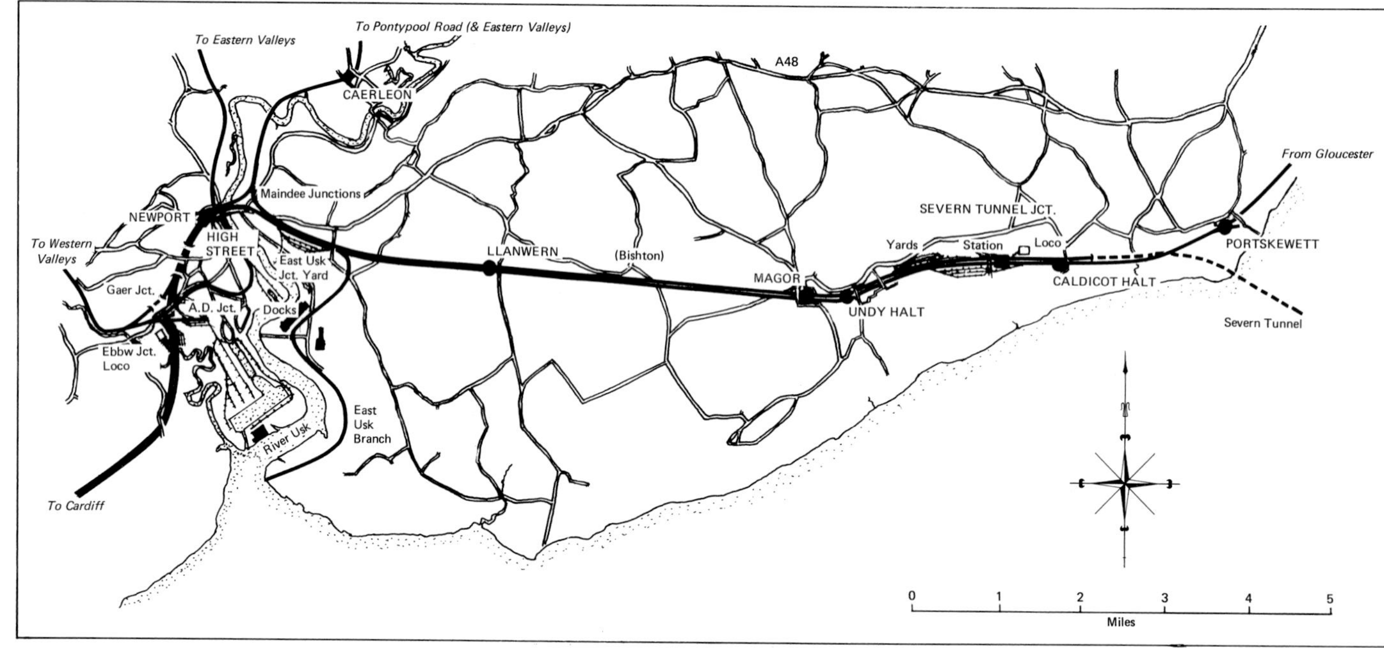

PREFACE

I always had a strong attraction to Newport. In addition to it being my mother's family home, its railway attraction was immense as it was the point where trains funnelled together to and from the Cardiff direction and the Western Valleys before the lines fanned out after the critical mile or so through High Street Station. The succession of freight services through the area was one of the phenomena of the Western Region, and the overlapping platforms at the station presented excellent vantage points for action photography.

Severn Tunnel Junction was a place to visit on a warm day – when there was no cold wind sweeping across the flatlands. I made several visits there, especially to the cutting leading to and from the Severn Tunnel, where there was good scope for photographing both passenger and freight services, the latter double-headed for their passage through the Tunnel.

The level of activity over the stretch of line from the Severn Tunnel to Newport made it a mecca for photography in the steam age. Newport is still a focal point for freight activity, and I hope that this book gives a clear representation of what it was like when steam traction was still dominant during the 'fifties and early 'sixties.

John Hodge
Haywards Heath West Sussex

ISBN 1 874103 76 3

Designed by Paul Karau
Printed by Amadeus Press, Cleckheaton

Published by
WILD SWAN PUBLICATIONS LTD.
1-3 Hagbourne Road, Didcot, Oxon, OX11 8DP

The complications of multiple train regulation is illustrated in this view of High Street on 18th April 1961. Before the changes of 1961, the signalmen in Maindee Junction East, Newport East and West, and Gaer Junction boxes were involved in crossing passenger and freight trains over between the Main and Relief lines to gain access to their platforms or lines or to the various routes immediately beyond. This view shows Radyr's '72XX' 2–8–2T No.7205 on the Up Main road, with a train for Severn Tunnel Jct or Salisbury passing a down freight headed by Aberdare's '28XX' 2–8–0 No.2886 on the Down Main. The '28' had caught up with Canton 'Castle' No.5048 *Earl of Devon* on the 11.55 a.m. Paddington to Pembroke Dock, standing at platform 6 (former 1/2), which had taken precedence over it at Maindee East. Having run through the station, the '28' would be routed across from the Main to Relief lines (old designation), either at Newport West or Gaer Jct., in order to gain access to the Gaer branch beyond. Although the 'Main' and 'Relief lines had been redesignated the previous weekend, and the platforms renumbered, use of the former down platform was as yet unchanged from former days.

HISTORICAL OVERVIEW

The South Wales Railway opened its broad gauge line between Chepstow, Newport, Cardiff and Swansea on 18th June 1850. When the SWR's plans for a railway through Newport were produced in the early 1840s, they provoked huge local opposition and vast sums had to be spent by the promoters in canvassing the scheme before it was finally accepted. One of the main concerns was the routeing of the railway along the coast between Newport and Chepstow; the principal rivals proposed an alternative route following the Usk Valley through Caerleon to Monmouth and thence to Gloucester, but this was rejected by the promoters.

The SWR always had very close ties with the Great Western Railway which saw the new line as part of its grandiose plan to link London with Southern Ireland as well as South Wales. The GWR was very active in the promotion of the new broad gauge line, and the prospectus for the new venture was in fact issued from the GWR's London offices. This detailed a capital for the new company of £2.5m. in £50 shares, and said there was such overwhelming demand and support for the new line that the Bill for its creation was assured of being passed.

From the issue of the prospectus in the summer if 1844, the line between Chepstow and Swansea took less than six years to be authorised and built. There were three main works involved: the Newport bridge across the River Usk, the Newport Tunnel, and the Landore Viaduct across the River Tawe. The inaugural run on 18th June 1850 was made with two engines hauling the special train, with Brunel on the leading engine, each stop along the route from Chepstow to Swansea being greeted with great ceremony, particularly so, as 18th June was then celebrated as Waterloo Day. Luxury saloon cars were provided for the Directors and their ladies and guests, with open carriages (more akin to goods wagons) for the less favoured.

The service proper began the next day with four trains per day in both directions from Monday to Saturday and two on Sundays. Trains left Chepstow at 8.0 a.m., 12 noon, 4.30 p.m. and 7.0 p.m., the first and last calling at Portskewett. In the other direction, trains left Swansea at 7.0 a.m., 10.30 a.m., 2.0 p.m. and 6.0 p.m. The first train of the day westward and the last eastward were so-called Parliamentary trains, as they complied with Gladstone's Railway Act of 1844 which laid down that every railway company must run at least one train per day to provide passengers travelling third class with seats and covered accommodation, with fares not to exceed a penny per mile. On Sundays trains left both Chepstow and Swansea at 7.0 a.m. and 6.0 p.m., the evening train including third class accommodation. Greenwich time was kept at all stations, this being necessary as, in 1850, Cardiff was 12 mins in advance of London time, and Swansea 15 mins.

For a short time, the route remained isolated from the GWR's London line, though a step towards connection was taken on 19th September 1851, when a new section between Grange Court (the limit of the GW line) and Chepstow East was opened. The through link between Chepstow East and Chepstow, across a new bridge spanning the River Wye, was completed in July 1852 and from that time, through running became possible between London, Swindon, Gloucester and South Wales. Stations were opened by the SWR in the area at Portskewett (later for the ferry from New Passage, Bristol, in 1863), Magor, Llanwern and Newport, now with six passenger services per day in each direction, and a couple of additional trains each way to the west of Newport. Services were operated by GWR engines and stock (the coaches having much of the appearance of stage coaches about them, with luggage on the roof), though other staffing was provided by the SWR. In May 1853, the Great Western provided sixteen 'Priam' class passenger, five 'Fury' class goods and two 'Leo' tank engines for South Wales sheds, though others operated through from England.

Newport was developing as the principal outlet to the eastern part of the South Wales & Monmouthshire coalfield, with extensive dock facilities along the western bank of the River Usk, and the Alexandra Dock complex (North and South Docks) contained between the Ebbw and Usk Rivers, to the south of the town. The docks soon came third in the coal-exporting league in South Wales, a position they held up to the early 1930s, behind the two major facilities at Cardiff and Barry. In 1900, Newport exported 3½ million tons of coal and coke, a figure that rose gradually upwards to a peak of 6¾ million tons in 1923. However, by 1932, export coal had dropped to below its 1900 level, and never recovered. A heavy business in tinplates and galvanized sheets, iron and steelwork developed around the town, mostly on the east bank of the Usk; Newport became the epitome of a large town built around heavy industry.

At Newport, the SWR was joined (though not physically) with the Monmouthshire Railways and Canal Company's local railways, which had been developed from their existing tramroads as decreed by an Act of 1845, though progress had been slow. An improved tramroad service from Blaina to Newport using a terminus at Courtybella was introduced in December 1850, and extended to Dock Street in August, 1852. Meanwhile a standard gauge railway had opened from Pontypool Crane Street to a Newport station at Marshes Turnpike Gate in July 1852, extended to Mill Street in March 1853. The Blaina tramroad was converted into a standard gauge railway in May 1855, and a service from the Sirhowy Valley to Dock Street opened in 1865, by which time the Eastern Valley line had been extended back to Blaenavon. Three stations thus existed within Newport from mid-1850: the SWR line at High Street, and the MR & CC's Dock Street and Mill Street.

The South Wales Railway was amalgamated with the Great Western Railway in August 1863.

In May 1872, the broad gauge South Wales Main Line was converted to 'narrow' gauge, which thus became the standard, creating direct access to other parts of the country for its growing trade in minerals without the problems of transhipment previously caused by the change of gauge. Direct workings to the Midlands, North, South and West of England and to Scotland now became possible, though the broad gauge continued beyond Exeter until 1892. Much of the coal traffic originating in South Wales was carried by sea at this time, involving local movement to the ports along the Glamorgan and Monmouthshire coast.

The next significant addition to the main-line scene in the area was the opening of the GWR-sponsored Pontypool, Caerleon & Newport Railway on 17th September 1874. The origins of this went right back to the Newport, Abergavenny & Hereford Railway who, in 1854, opened the first stage of its line northwards from Pontypool (Coedygric) to meet up with the Hereford to Shrewsbury line. This new line provided through communication to and from the Midlands and the North via Hereford, Worcester or Shrewsbury, and enabled the Eastern Valley trains to run into High Street station instead of Mill Street, using a new section of line between Cwmbran and Llantarnam Jct. to link up with the Pontypool Crane Street and Blaenavon line.

In 1879, the GWR opened a direct link line between Park Junction and Gaer Junction through a new Gaer Tunnel, enabling trains running from the Western and Sirhowy Valleys to Dock Street to use the GWR station at High Street. However, for this to take place, considerable alterations to the layout were necessary at the main-line station. These were completed by 11th March 1880, when the Valley trains ran in alongside the main line at High Street, and Dock Street and Mill Street were closed as passenger stations.

These were momentous times in the railway history of South Wales, and on 1st September 1886 a new milestone was reached with the opening of the Severn Tunnel. Initially, only goods trains and passenger trains to and from Bristol used it. Soon afterwards, trains to and from London passed that way, routed via Bristol (Stapleton Road) and Bath, with a mileage from Newport to Paddington of 143½, as opposed to 158½ via Gloucester. Three months after the opening of the tunnel, a new station, Severn Tunnel Junction, was opened to traffic on 1st December 1886.

In the early 1890s, the main passenger services were mainly hauled by 'Barnum', 'Stella' and '3232' 2–4–0 classes, and around the turn of the century by 4–4–0s of the 'Duke', 'Bulldog' and 'Atbara' classes. The first of the 'modern' classes to appear in South Wales were London 'Saints' on Irish boat trains during 1905, consolidated by the allocation of 'Saints' to Cardiff in 1907. In 1906, the prototype of the 'Star' class – No.40 – was also recorded on New Milford boat trains, and examples of the class were allocated to Canton from 1908.

The final stage of route development affecting South Wales took place on 1st May 1903, when the Badminton route between Patchway and Wootton Bassett was opened to freight traffic, with passenger trains following on 1st July. This cut-off route further reduced the mileage between Newport and Paddington to 133½.

Although the Severn Tunnel had substantially reduced the distance between South Wales and London, and enabled trains to avoid the gradients on the Gloucester route – particularly Sapperton – the tunnel itself was a cause of some concern from an operating point of view. The gradients within the tunnel were 1 in 100 on the English side and 1 in 90 on the Welsh, which initially limited the weight which could be hauled on the goods trains using it.

Development of heavy goods engines to replace the various 0–6–0 classes then working the heavy coal and other traffic had also begun. In 1899, the first of the 'Krugers' appeared on South Wales coal trains, followed soon afterwards by the 2–6–0 'Aberdares', and finally, in late 1905, the first production engines of the '2800' class 2–8–0s, which did much to transform the main-line coal and general goods traffic. Though most of the new 2–8–0s were based at the London end initially, examples were allocated to Severn Tunnel and Aberdare in 1905/6, and to Newport and Pontypool Road soon afterwards; the pattern of freight motive power was thus largely set for the next sixty years. In order to convey a realistic load through the tunnel, banking was resorted to at an early stage.

The section between Severn Tunnel West and East boxes was some 4 miles 54 chains. Intense occupation of the tunnel was normal, and with two engines hauling most goods trains, ventilation conditions were poor. During the early 1920s, in an endeavour to overcome the problems, the GWR considered electrification of the existing tunnel section, and also the provision of a duplicate tunnel; however, the former was considered too costly, and the latter would have perpetuated many of the problems of the existing bore. Serious consideration was therefore given to the construction of a bridge to ease the traffic problems through the tunnel.

The principle of providing a bridge across the Severn was not new. Between 1845 and 1896, no less than 18 schemes had been promoted to cross the Severn to the south of Gloucester, of which 13 proposed the use of a 'viaduct'. Of the 18, only the Severn Bridge (Midland Railway, near Sharpness, 1879) and the Severn Tunnel came to fruition. The proposed new bridge would cross from near Oldbury-on-Severn, pass over the Gloucester line to the south of Chepstow, then turn south and descend to a junction with that line just to the north of Portskewett. On the English side, a new railway from Westerleigh was envisaged, with a short connecting line northwards from Patchway to join it. The bridge would hold the advantages of much easier gradients (1 in 240 on both sides was possible), allowing the passage of heavy trains without the delays and difficulties associated with banking, a greater flow of traffic at faster speeds, and at a cost far less than a duplicate tunnel. The provision of an integral road span was also put forward. This proposal was estimated to cost over £5 million, and was not taken up. The tunnel thus continued as a bottleneck to traffic for another forty or 50 years, until the reduction in the level of rail freight traffic in the 1960s and 70s removed the problem.

From 1924, Old Oak Common 'Castles' could be seen working through Newport on the Irish boat trains and excursions from London. By 1927 they were working daily through to Carmarthen, but it was not until 1928/9 that examples of the class were allocated to Cardiff (Canton) to replace 'Stars' (back at Canton from 1926) on London diagrams; the engines handled the London trains superbly over the following 30 or so years.

Quadrupling of the line between Severn Tunnel Jct. and Newport had been deemed necessary before the First World War in some quarters of the GWR's organisation, though for various reasons nothing was done. It was not until 1941 that quadrupling took place, with the additional pressures of wartime traffic requirements forcing the point.

Though the level of goods traffic reduced slightly after the war, greater flows of heavy freight developed during the 1950s, including iron and steel, tinplate, oil, and imported ores, as well as such new commodities as banana traffic. With the increase in passenger traffic during the 1950s, especially on summer Saturdays, the quadruple lines were kept well occupied. The Cardiff Division, which latterly managed the line from Fishguard to Severn Tunnel, was becoming very concerned at the delays to line occupation caused at stations from where there was little originating revenue, and on 12th September 1960 closed the station at Llanwern, together with its goods facilities, followed by the passenger stations at Magor and Undy Halt in November 1964. Magor yard was kept open for materials used in the building of the M4 Motorway – especially trainloads of cement – finally closing in July 1965.

The section of line was, however, to be transformed by the building of the Richard Thomas & Baldwin's Spencer Steelworks at Llanwern in 1961. For the practical reception of large volumes of iron ore from Newport Docks and coking coal from the Western Valley pits, it was necessary to redesign the track layout from Alexandra Dock Jct. to Llanwern, and also to provide a flyover for outwards (eastbound) finished traffic to leave the plant and gain access to the up relief line.

As things stood, these freight trains would have needed to cross all lines to get from the up relief into the plant at Llanwern – a patently impractical position, as the delays to passenger services would have been considerable. The only practical solution lay in redesignating the running lines, so that the up and down reliefs were located on the south side throughout between A.D. Jct. and Llanwern, as indeed they had been since quadrupling between Cardiff and A.D. Jct. in 1898. The order of tracks to the east of Newport (from the north side) had previously been Up Relief, Up Main, Down Main, Down Relief. In order to accommodate the steelworks traffic, the Up Relief line now became the Up Main, the Up Main became the Down Main, and the former Down Main the Up Relief, producing a need for considerable upgrading of the condition of the former Up Relief. The re-designation of tracks was accompanied by reversible working between Gaer Jct. and Newport East, and the whole was covered by new Multiple Aspect Signalling, one new panel box eventually replacing all the manual boxes in the Newport area.

With dieselisation, trainloads as well as train speeds increased, and the level of occupation of the section benefited accordingly. The changing pattern of freight traffic, hugely influenced by the disengagement from goods sundries traffic in 1972 and from wagon load traffic in 1976, had a devastating effect on Severn Tunnel Marshalling Yard, leading to its complete closure in the 1980s.

In later years, the closure of most of the South Wales coalfield also meant that Llanwern's coking coal requirement has been met by imported coal, initially from Newport, Cardiff and Barry Docks, but latterly from Avonmouth Dock, and especially the deep water port

Reading 'Manor' No.7813 *Freshford Manor* emerging from the western portal of the Severn Tunnel on the 1 in 90 climb towards the junction with a train of potatoes from the Channel Islands (telegraph code 'Perpot' – 'Special potato or perishable train leaving Weymouth at ...') in June 1964. The freight was a class '4', formerly 'C' vacuum, with the vehicles piped throughout the train, and the automatic brake operative on at least half of them. This service is a descendant of the very first Great Western express vacuum goods service into South Wales – the 9.55 p.m. Paddington (balance 6.30 p.m. Swansea) – in September 1905. The vacuum train system expanded quickly, and a year later the services had been joined by Paddington & Fishguard and Bordesley & Cardiff trains. By 1960, the class '4' trains were specified as a maximum of 50 vehicles (13-ton), with a maximum permitted speed of 55 mph. Potatoes also flowed in the opposite direction from late spring, with regular special trains from Pembrokeshire for Paddington, Birmingham and Shrewsbury.

at Port Talbot, from where iron ore has also been supplied in 3,000-ton trains. The recent announcement by Corus of the curtailment of steel making at Llanwern adds a final but unwelcome tail to the story.

THE SEVERN TUNNEL

Work originally began on the building of the Severn Tunnel in 1873, but after six years with little progress to be seen, and with the River Severn defeating all attempts to be mastered by the original contractors, the GWR turned to Thomas Walker, a railway engineer of considerable standing in several countries, to re-submit his tender for taking over the work. This tender for £948,959 had previously been rejected as being too high, but the GWR's consulting engineer, Sir John Hawkshaw, now convinced the GW Board that if they wished to see progress made on the project, it should be handed over to Walker.

When Walker arrived on the scene at the end of 1879, he found the project at a standstill; most of the men employed by the previous contractor had gone off to find other work and most of the installations and machinery, which had proved to be inadequate to the task, were standing idle. On being awarded the contract, Walker immediately ordered larger capacity pumps and sank four new shafts. He drew up new plans to site the tunnel an additional 15 feet below the deepest channel of the river, known as 'The Shoots', to prevent flooding of the works which had previously taken place. By dropping the line of the tunnel to 65 feet below the lowest part of the river bed, the gradient on the Welsh side became 1 in 90 rather than 1 in 100.

On the occasion that the tunnel shafts had previously flooded, the workers had fled to safety by whatever means possible, but in so doing had left an underground iron door open, the closure of which was critical to the resumption of the work. This was Walker's first major problem, and was overcome after several attempts by a very experienced diver named Lambert, who used the new compressed air back-pack in place of air supply hoses. After exactly a year with Walker in charge, the workings were clear of water, and he first constructed a strong wall leading westward from the original shaft to control the Great Spring, which had been the cause of the previous flooding. However, progress in this direction was cut short by a strike of part of his workforce, resentful of their longer working day of 10 hours plus 2 hours meal breaks in place of the previous 8 hours, and of the men Walker had brought in from a previous project. Walker used the strike to his advantage to rid himself of several troublemakers, and thereafter good working relations were restored. Walker had already provided well for his workforce with a new village at Sudbrook, together with a school, church and other local amenities.

By October 1881, the east and west end bores had been joined, and the first of the Sudbrook fans commissioned to create through ventilation in place of the previous compressed air. Progress was not without other problems, such as the panic created one night at the end of 1882 when a group of workmen told Walker that the water was again flooding in, but were unable to give details. Walker himself went to investigate, and found the installation completely intact, though hundreds of men had fled from the tunnel. Though this was a false alarm, the Great Spring did burst in again during October 1883 and flooded the lower section of the Tunnel for a mile and a half, sweeping away men and equipment, though with no loss of human life. Only a week later, a high tide engulfed the Welsh end of the workings and the Marsh Shaft was flooded; though many men were trapped for several hours, all except one were rescued.

Walker's high-capacity pumps dealt effectively with both floods, and no further problems were encountered, enabling the tunnel to be virtually completed by the end of 1884. The final brickwork was completed by April 1885 and the tunnel pronounced ready for use by the end of that summer. The first train ran through on 5th September, conveying GWR officials, including Sir Daniel Gooch. The first ordinary train passed through on 9th January 1886, a double-headed coal train from Aberdare to Southampton. Further work was, however, still required on the tunnel and the access cuttings, and it was not until 1st September 1886 that it was opened for goods traffic, and for passenger trains, initially between Cardiff and Bristol, on 1st December.

The final total cost for building the tunnel, including both the original contractor's abortive efforts and the successful Thomas Walker project, was just over £1.8m. Such was his standing that, while engaged on the tunnel project, Walker was called to a board meeting of the Barry Dock and Railway Directors, and was awarded the contract to build their new dock and, railway.

On the Welsh side of the Severn, the tunnel line descended eastwards from Severn Tunnel Jct. East in a cutting, on a parallel course to the Gloucester line, entering the western portal of the tunnel after ¾-mile. Shortly afterwards it turned to the south-east, passing under the Gloucester line, then continued its descent under land

A late-running Shrewsbury 'Castle' No.5050 *Earl of St. Germans* climbing away from the tunnel on Saturday, 14th May 1960 with train No.949, the 8.0 a.m. Plymouth to Liverpool. This service carried a restaurant car for Liverpool, a through portion from Kingswear (depart 8.0 a.m.) to Manchester at the rear, and a through Brake Composite from Plymouth to Glasgow at the head. The 8.0 a.m. Plymouth was the return working of a double-home turn between Shrewsbury and Newton Abbot, shared by engines and men from those sheds. The balancing train was the 9.5 a.m. Liverpool to Plymouth, worked southwards from Shrewsbury (depart 11.18 a.m.) by a Shrewsbury engine and men on Mondays, Wednesdays and Fridays, returning with the 8.0 a.m. Plymouth on Tuesdays, Thursdays and Saturdays (as seen here). The train behind the express was the 11.30 a.m. Severn Tunnel Jct. to Avonmouth, hauled by '2251' class 0–6–0 No.2292, piloted by 2–6–2T, No.4156. Tanks belonging to the Imperial Smelting Corporation (National Smelting Co.) can be seen in the up train, the nearest marked for the conveyance of sulphuric acid. The National Smelting Company was to be found at Newport, Six Pit Jct. (Llansamlet, near Swansea) and Avonmouth (Hallen Marsh) in the local area.

Following the late-running 8.0 a. m. Plymouth to Liverpool train out of the tunnel on 14th May 1960 was the down 'Pembroke Coast Express', the 10.55 am. Paddington, hauled by Landore 'Castle' No.7028 *Cadbury Castle*. This was the fastest train of the day between Paddington and Cardiff with a run of 2½ hours, calling at Newport for two minutes en route. It was critical that this train had a clear run through the tunnel, and signalmen were to keep all down freights well clear for the train's passage; judging by the number of times the 10.55 was a few minutes late into Cardiff, this was no easy task. The train conveyed a dining car for luncheons (at 9s 6d) as far as Swansea, where the car and its portion were detached; an hour later, they were attached to the up 'Pembroke Coast Express', which left Swansea at 3.45 p.m. No.7028 went to Landore as new in June 1950, and remained there until the closure of the shed for dieselisation in June 1961, when it was transferred to Llanelly. The engine had been in traffic for six months after a heavy general repair when this photograph was taken.

'28XX' 2–8–0 No.2861 pulling up the bank past Severn Tunnel West box with a class 'F' train of mineral empties on 14th May 1960, with a few wooden-bodied vehicles still in evidence. Unassisted, the '28XX' could haul 76 empty wagons between Pilning and Severn Tunnel Jct., and this load could be taken by special provision, although 65 vehicles was the 'operational' maximum for the tunnel section. An 'F' class service was scheduled for 14 minutes along the five-mile section between the Tunnel East and West boxes. The engine was stationed at Severn Tunnel Jct., and its load was probably destined for Rogerstone or Cardiff. Empties were returned to South Wales under the instructions of the Central Wagon Authority from Acton, Reading, Swindon, Tavistock Jct., Hackney, Exeter or Bristol in train-loads, or marshalled within mixed services, depending upon numbers involved.

On Saturday, 14th May 1960, this 'Hall' was descending towards Severn Tunnel West box and the tunnel with the 8.30 a.m. Carmarthen to Bristol service. During 1959/60, the turn was worked by a Taunton engine, and No.5999 *Wollaton Hall* often worked on the train, though perhaps not in this instance. In contrast to the heavy freight services, an express passenger would occupy about five minutes in the section between West and East boxes.

and river. Having climbed from under the centre of the River Severn, the line emerged into daylight on the English side some 7,668 yards from the western portal.

In order to achieve maximum loading of trains, banking was necessary through the tunnel, and this was initially performed by 0–6–0 saddle and pannier tanks of the '2721' and '1854' classes. Following the allocation of the first two members of the '3150' class in December 1907, the number of 2–6–2Ts gradually increased, and they came to dominate banking work over the next 50 years, though initially most were of the '3100' Class. The benefit of piloting with these engines was substantial – a '28XX' engine itself could convey 40 loaded coal wagons eastward through the tunnel and up to Patchway, but with assistance from a '3150' (group 'D') engine, the permitted load rose to 65; banking was therefore necessary in most instances to raise the single engine load of the tunnel section to a realistic working level for routes beyond.

'Castle' class No.4076 *Carmarthen Castle* climbing past Severn Tunnel West box on 14th May 1960 with train No.709, the 8.55 a.m. Paddington to Pembroke Dock. This train comprised a section for Pembroke Dock at the front, a portion for Neyland in the centre, and one for Swansea (including dining car) at the rear. The silver-painted buffers were a feature of Landore 'Castles' at this time, and been introduced because Landore drivers on London turns had complained of the difficulty of finding their engines amongst all the other 'Castles' on shed at Old Oak. The Landore shedmaster had directed that his 'Castles' should be thus painted, in order to 'stand out from the common herd'. No.4076 became a Landore engine in December 1957, after eight years at Chester, and was to remain in the area at Landore, Llanelly and Neath until withdrawal in February 1963. Up to 1958, the 8.55 a.m. Paddington had carried the number '163', and from 1960, 'F15'.

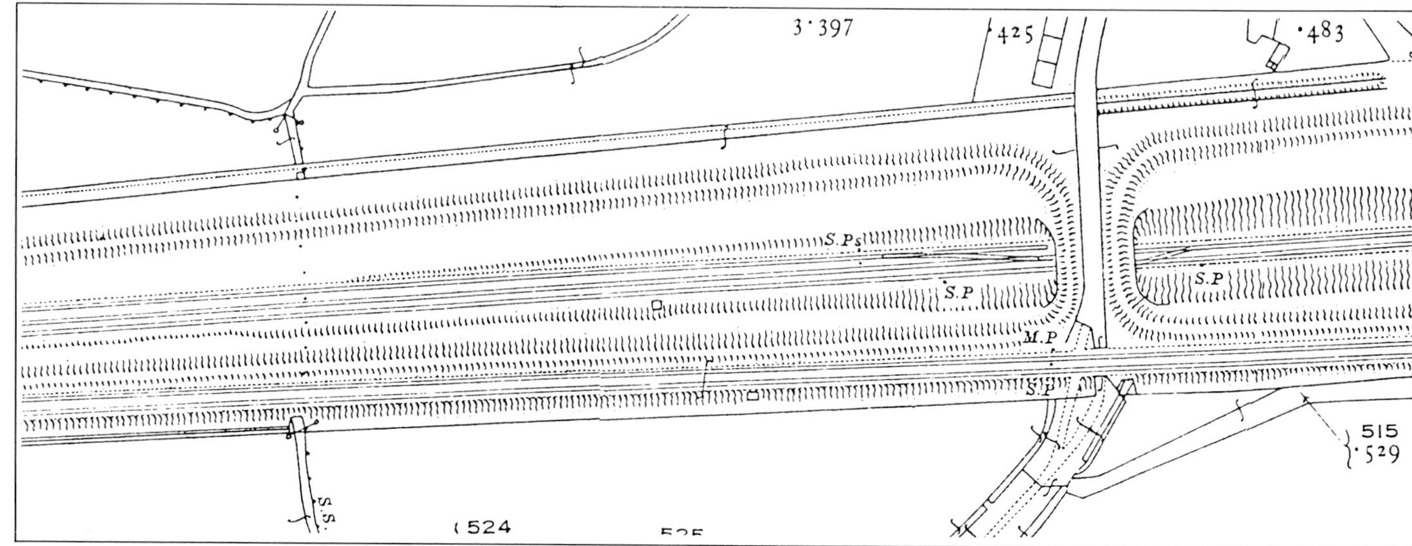

The car service through the Severn Tunnel – advertised in the timetables as 'avoiding the long road detour via Gloucester' – was introduced by the Great Western around 1921 between Patchway, Pilning and Severn Tunnel Jct. Early conveyance was by open or covered trucks (at the owner's preference, with the latter a more expensive option), with specially-fitted carriage trucks introduced in 1924. In this 1964 view, a down service is seen passing Severn Tunnel West box with a 2–6–2T hauling a three-wagon train, and a coach for the passengers.

Canton 'Britannia' No.70016 *Ariel* with train No.048, the 8.0 a.m. Neyland to Paddington on Saturday, 14th May 1960, seen from Severn Tunnel West box, looking towards the Junction. The engine lacks the normal Canton lustre and may have been a last-minute replacement for the 12 noon Cardiff turn. An ex-LNER coach is seen leading the formation, and odd examples of these were quite a familiar sight on South Wales expresses for strengthening purposes around this time. The bridge seen here conveyed the roadway from Caldicot village onto Roggiett and Caldicot Moors, passing underneath the Gloucester line just off to the left, where it also served nearby Caldicot Halt.

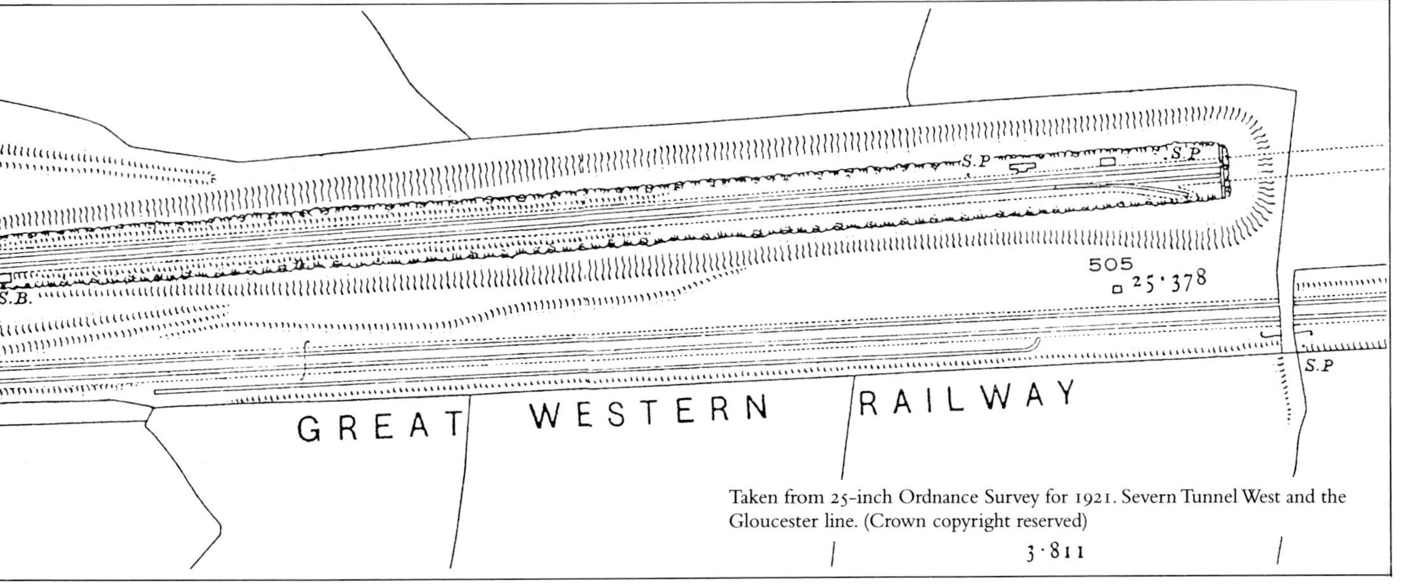

Taken from 25-inch Ordnance Survey for 1921. Severn Tunnel West and the Gloucester line. (Crown copyright reserved)

No.7019 *Fowey Castle* (of Bath Road shed) running down the incline towards the tunnel with a twelve-coach 11.10 a.m. Swansea to Penzance (No.433) on Saturday, 14th May 1960. The service conveyed coaches for Paignton, and a buffet car to Plymouth. Through coaches were running between South Wales and the West Country by the summer of 1900, attached at Bristol to the 10.35 a.m. Paddington express. With the subsequent opening of the Berks & Hants route to the west, many of the fast London trains were diverted away from the Bristol route, and coaches from Cardiff to Newquay and Penzance were, by 1909, conveyed instead by the 10.0 a.m. Wolverhampton and 10.35 a.m. Penzance through trains from and to Bristol. Daily through trains were running between Cardiff and Paignton by 1924.

Oxford's class '4' 4–6–0 No.75007 at Caldicot with the class 'H' Llantrisant to Pensnett (West Midlands) coke on 14th May 1960, routed via Gloucester, Cheltenham and Honeybourne. Caldicot Halt was opened on 12th September 1932, and in 1963 still had 14 trains each way calling daily. The bracket signal for the up goods loops on the up tunnel line can be seen below the station nameboard on the right.

To the west of the Caldicot road bridge, two lengthy goods loops (of 68-wagon capacity) were provided to accommodate up goods trains awaiting passage through the tunnel. The first loop was added around 1901 and the second in 1942 to enable the passage of heavy wartime traffic. In these views, Severn Tunnel Junction's '51XX' 2–6–2T No.5110 was assisting Ebbw Junction's '9F' 2–10–0 No.92000 with the class 'H' 7.50 a.m. Rogerstone to Tavistock Jct. on 14th May 1960. The train conveyed coal from the Aberdare and Western Valleys to Taunton, Exeter, Newton Abbot and Tavistock Jct yards (also for connecting services), and included loco coal for Newton Division sheds as required. The train was awaiting the road in the first two views, and is seen pulling out onto the up main from No.1 loop in the last. The train engine retained its 'H' class lamps for the journey through the 'hole', whilst the '51' carried its target ('T3') and local lamp.

A view taken from the water tank steps at Severn Tunnel Jct. shed in June 1964, looking east along the tunnel (left) and Gloucester (right) lines with No.6958 *Oxburgh Hall* making its way along No.1 goods loop with the 7.25 p.m. Magor to Hoo Jct. (nr. Gravesend) empty cement cars on the tunnel route. This train was routed via Old Oak, though it had earlier run via Salisbury. The Caldicot roadbridge can be seen in the distance on the tunnel line, with the west portal of the tunnel beyond. It was almost another two miles underground before the line passed under the west bank of the River Severn at Sudbrook. To the right of the roadbridge, Caldicot Halt can just be seen, alongside the rear of a down freight on the Gloucester line as it was entering the reception loop for the down hump yard.

A sign of modernisation, with the down 'Blue Pullman' – 4.55 p.m. Paddington to Swansea – approaching Severn Tunnel Jct. East. Before the 'Blue Pullman' replaced the steam train on the 'South Wales Pullman' in 1961, the timings – 8.50 a.m. Paddington to Swansea (due 1.10 p.m.) and the 4.30 p.m. Swansea return (Paddington 8.45) – produced poor revenue. It was therefore decided to change the basis of operation, and the train ran 6.40 a.m. from Swansea, leaving Cardiff at 8.0 a.m. (due Paddington 10.15 a.m.), in which format it was an immediate success, with all seats taken on most days of the week. The return train, 4.55 p.m. Paddington (due Swansea 8.40), was not so popular, as many businessmen returned on earlier services. To the right of the Pullman, the goods running loop and seven reception sidings for the down hump yard can be seen beyond the Gloucester main lines. In contrast to the tunnel route, the Gloucester line ran virtually level towards Portskewett.

SEVERN TUNNEL JUNCTION

SEVERN TUNNEL JUNCTION ENGINE SHED

The first engine shed at Severn Tunnel Jct. was a small, two-road structure, located at the east end of the station on the up side. In January 1901, this housed ten '2721', two '1854' and one '1076' class 0–6–0 tanks for shunting and banking, a couple of '517' class 0–4–2Ts for passenger work, and a '79' class 0–6–0 for goods. The '2721s' were reduced over the following years in favour of more '1854s' for banking duties. The shed saw the arrival of '28XXs' in 1906, when four members of the class stayed for short periods in the early part of the year, and four on a permanent basis in the latter half, whilst three 'Aberdares' were also present. This influx indicated the increasing importance of the shed for heavy freight work, another aspect that would enlarge significantly over the years.

A new shed to replace the 1886 depot was opened in the early part of 1908, providing full facilities for 'the increase in numbers of large engines hauling the heavy coal trains from South Wales' – as reported by the *Great Western Magazine*. The shed was the standard 210ft by 66ft four-road structure, with accommodation alongside the northern edge shown as 50ft of stores, 32ft of offices (etc.) and 103ft for fitters (etc.), each 14ft wide; the south wall of the shed was

Old Oak 'Castle' No.7029 *Clun Castle* at Severn Tunnel Jct. East on one of its 'end of steam' runs; this was an LCGB special, 9.25 a.m. Paddington to Shrewsbury (via the North & West route) on Sunday, 21st June 1964. The special departed from Paddington at 9.25 a.m. behind No.7808, and after a tour of Swindon works, was taken on to Shrewsbury by No.7029. The train was topping the 1 in 90 climb from the tunnel, with no significant gradients onwards to Newport. Over on the left is Severn Tunnel Jct. shed, with the two original bays of the 1908 shed and the 1931 extension on their right. The water tank steps on the left were an excellent photographic venue for long views over the countryside to the east.

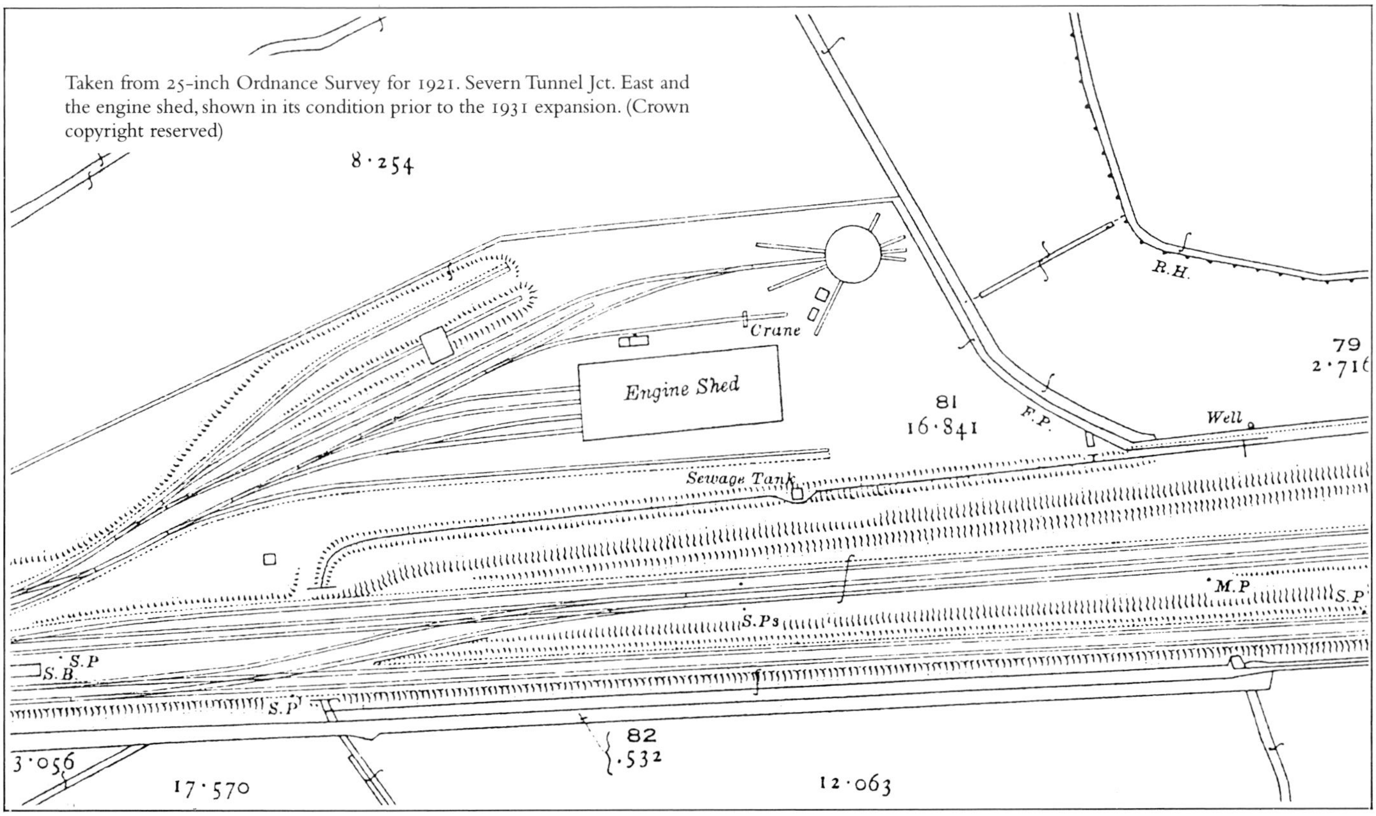

Taken from 25-inch Ordnance Survey for 1921. Severn Tunnel Jct. East and the engine shed, shown in its condition prior to the 1931 expansion. (Crown copyright reserved)

Severn Tunnel Jct. shed, on 13th September 1953. This shows the western face of the facilities, and illustrates, from the left, the coal stage, ash shelter, lifting shop (in the distance), offices, and the six-road shed.

'so erected as to allow of the shed being extended to eight roads if found necessary later on.' Other facilities found on the northern side were the sand furnace, which measured 17ft by 13ft, beyond which was the 65ft standard 'over-girder' turntable. The coal stage nearby measured 30ft by 30ft, with a 42,000-gallon storage tank over, 'divided into two parts for hard and soft water.' Engine pits were provided for maintenance, those within the shed being 190ft, and on the shed roads outside 40ft. Another 130ft pit was located in front of the coal stage, and 132ft on the outgoing road from the turntable. Both yard and shed were lit by acetylene gas. A building for two further roads was added alongside in 1931, at which time many other improvements were effected.

As a shed concerned largely with goods duties, Severn Tunnel Jct. in 1939 housed around 70 engines, with '28XX', '30XX', '43XX', '72XX', '3150', '56XX' and 0–6–0PTs on 32 freight turns. In addition, there were the nine banking turns worked by the '3150' engines, and 11 shunting and pilot turns operated by '56XX', '57XX', '74XX', '1854' and '2021' classes. Two local passenger turns were worked by '3150' and '51XX' 2–6–2Ts, and a 'Bulldog'; these included the depot's only 'main line' duty, which ran from Severn Tunnel Jct. to Chepstow, thence to Cardiff and back to Chepstow and return. In September 1940 'Saint' No. 2922 *Saint Gabriel* was allocated to work this turn, until November 1944, when the turn was extended to Swansea.

By Nationalisation, the depot (now coded 86E) had acquired four 'Granges' for freight work in addition to No.2952 *Twineham Court* (from November 1947 to August 1951) which had taken over the Chepstow, Cardiff & Swansea passenger service. There were now seventeen '28XXs', including four oil-burners, a 'WD', and two '43XXs' for main-line freight, with Avonmouth services worked by two '2301' Class 0–6–0s. Services within South Wales were handled by ten '72XX's supported by four '42XXs'. There were thirty 2–6–2Ts for piloting through the tunnel, local freight and other turns, and nine '56XXs' for local freight turns. Yard shunting was carried out by ten 0–6–0PTs and two ex-B&M engines. The Monmouth line services were worked by 0–4–2T No.3575. A total of 93 engines were allocated.

Severn Tunnel Jct. shed in 1959 was provided with around fifty '28XX', '9F', '43XX', '42XX', '2251' and '56XX' engines for 38 goods and shunting turns, eleven '51s' and five '61s' for banking, passenger and other duties. 0–6–0 tank engines were employed on yard shunting. In the changeover from steam to diesel, Severn Tunnel Jct. was one of the last sheds to close on the Western Region, in October 1965, though a small diesel servicing depot continued the association with motive power.

'51XX' 2–6–2T No.5181 standing alongside the coal stage on 30th August 1959. This engine was transferred to Severn Tunnel Jct. in February 1958 after 27 years in the Wolverhampton Division, though Severn Tunnel Jct. always had one or two for passenger duties from the 1930s. A larger number were transferred in to replace withdrawn engines of the ageing '3150' class, which, since the latter 1920s, had expanded in numbers at the shed to perform the lion's share of banking duties through the 'hole'. Due to this work, these engines were never cleaned, and had the ignominious accolade of being the dirtiest engines on the Western Region, although they were always kept in good mechanical order. As at many other places before and during the Second World War, Severn Tunnel Junction's coal stage was extended using corrugated iron sheeting, seen here to the right of the loco. This gave additional loading stages on each side of the structure.

The west face of Severn Tunnel Jct. shed on 23rd September 1962, showing the offices, the 1908 four-road structure to the left, and the two-road 1931 addition to the right.

'28XX' No.2818, from Neath, outside the shed on 14th September 1963. Her mileage – 1,584,890 – was the highest of the class, and on account of this the engine was preserved at the NRM. The engine retained its straight front ends to the footplate, as built, one of several early '28s' (of the 2800–30 series) to do so. There were four water columns serving the front area of the shed, supplied from the large tank (of the usual 42,000 gallon capacity) over the coal stage, seen in the background.

No.6926 *Holkham Hall* of Tyseley shed (chalked '2A', the change of code occurring that month) seen on the northernmost shed road, alongside the office extension, on 14th September 1963. This engine remained in service until May 1965, after which it went to join many other such engines in the yard at Banbury for disposal.

The eastern facade of Severn Tunnel Jct. shed on 30th August 1959, with 86E's '2251' class 0–6–0 No.2231 and '56XX' 0–6–2T No.6672 on display. The shed's '2251s' were used on Avonmouth trains at this time. By this time, the shed comprised six through roads, two more being added in a building extension (the nearest structure) to the four original in 1931. At the same time, the original dead-end shed was opened out at its east end, with new through roads leading to the north and south of the buildings to provide access to the west end and the main lines.

No.92216 standing on a road to the south side of the shed buildings, alongside the 1931 extension structure, on 14th September 1963. The first '9Fs', Nos.92000–07, appeared at Ebbw Jct. in 1954, but were stored for modifications initially. Double-chimney 2–10–0 '9Fs' Nos.92203–92250 were first allocated to the Western Region in 1958, and by early 1960, there were 14 examples of these shared between Canton and Ebbw Jct. sheds, along with six of the earlier engines; they were making a considerable impact on the heavy freight scene, not to mention giving sprightly performances on summer Saturday through passenger workings.

2–8–0T No.5235 and 2–8–2T No.7245 outside the lifting shop at Severn Tunnel Jct shed on 26th April 1964. This standard structure was located immediately to the north of the main shed, and was representative of many that were built during the war years to allow running repairs for engines to take place at a greater number of locations.

A car carrier train for Pilning (or Patchway) standing at the Up Tunnel platform with a single coach and three vehicles for the motors, c.1963. The engine was '51XX' 2–6–2T No.4159, transferred to Severn Tunnel Jct in May 1962, and moved on to Wolverhampton in June 1964.

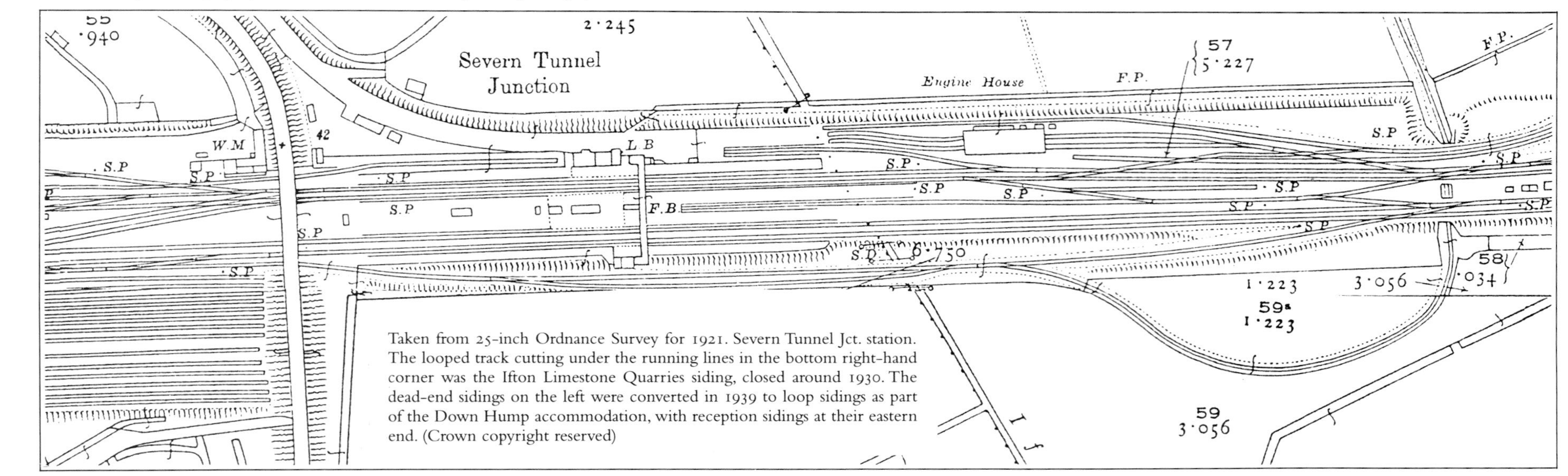

Taken from 25-inch Ordnance Survey for 1921. Severn Tunnel Jct. station. The looped track cutting under the running lines in the bottom right-hand corner was the Ifton Limestone Quarries siding, closed around 1930. The dead-end sidings on the left were converted in 1939 to loop sidings as part of the Down Hump accommodation, with reception sidings at their eastern end. (Crown copyright reserved)

PASSENGER STATION AND YARDS

The station at Severn Tunnel Junction was constructed on the southern outskirts of the small village of Roggiett, some 2¾ miles west of Portskewett, and opened for passenger traffic on 1st December 1886. It comprised three platforms, with four through faces: two outermost single-face platforms with an island platform in the centre, serving the two pairs of running lines. These roads joined to form double track to the west of the station. There were bays at the eastern ends of both the northerly and island platforms.

During the late 19th century, Severn Tunnel Junction was the point at which up freight services had their loads inspected, adjusted and reduced prior to entering the tunnel, whilst down trains from the tunnel had their loads augmented before proceeding westwards. For these purposes, marshalling sidings were provided, and located to the west of the station on both sides of the main line.

There were regular additions and improvements to yard facilities at Severn Tunnel Jct. In 1895, and again in 1900, additional sidings

On Thursday, 27th June 1957, Old Oak's No.7017 *G. J. Churchward* passing East box and approaching the station with the 11.55 a.m. Paddington to Pembroke Dock service, train No.167. The engine worked this train as far as Swansea, and at that time was scheduled to return the following morning with the 3.55 a.m. Fishguard to Paddington service. As the latter train did not call at Swansea, taking the District line via Felin Fran instead, the engine change was effected at Llanelly, giving the 'Castle' over five hours at the head of that train to London. The loco coal wagons to the left of the tunnel lines were awaiting use on shed.

Train 'V95', the 12.20 p.m. Manchester (Piccadilly) to Plymouth, at Severn Tunnel Jct. station behind 'King' No.6023 *King Edward II*, scheduled for a 5.10 p.m. departure for Temple Meads and the West. This was part of a turn for the Canton 'King' which involved the 8.55 a.m. Cardiff to Manchester (as far as Shrewsbury), the Plymouth train from Shrewsbury to Bristol, the 12 noon Penzance to Crewe train as far as Pontypool Road, finishing with the 12.5 a.m. Pontypool Road to Cardiff Many Severn Tunnel Jct. train crews travelled 'on the cushions' in many of the services that called. The substantial enclosed footbridge connecting the three platforms perhaps gave the impression of a station rather more important than it actually was. With little habitation nearby, Severn Tunnel Jct. was served regularly only by some cross-country expresses, and local services between Gloucester or Bristol and South Wales, its function being more of an interchange than an originating station.

Canton '28XX' No.2874 moving off the Down Gloucester line onto the goods loop at the west end of the station with a class 'H' train of iron ore, from Banbury to Guest, Keens at Cardiff Docks on Thursday, 27th June 1957. The Cardiff '28s' were additionally used for heavy trains to Saltney, Bordesley, Yarnton, the West Country and London at this time.

Auto 0–6–0PT No.5417 (of Gloucester shed) at the Down Gloucester line platform with 'The Severn Rambler', a Gloucester Railway Society tour of the Severn lines on 20th April 1958; this special had previously arrived from Gloucester behind 4–4–0 No.9017, and had just completed its branch line exploration. At this time, the Wye Valley auto services between Newport, Chepstow and Monmouth were still running, though their days were numbered; these usually comprised a '14XX' 0–4–2T and a couple of trailers. This pair provide examples of both compartment and saloon designs.

The Wye Valley diesel railcar No.21 standing at the Down Gloucester platform with a service from Monmouth and Chepstow on 21st March 1953; this car was one of the Dia.A1 series (Nos. 19–33), and was allocated to Newport during 1952–55. Leaving Ebbw Jct. at 6.35 a.m., the duty started with the 7.5 a.m. Newport to Monmouth (Troy), followed by one return trip from Monmouth to Chepstow, then the 11.50 a.m. Monmouth to Newport. The afternoon sequence started with the 1.45 pm. Newport, then the 3.55 p.m. Monmouth to Severn Tunnel Jct., the 5.0 p.m. back to Monmouth, 6.6 p.m. Monmouth to Severn Tunnel Jct., 7.10 p.m. thence to Chepstow and the 7.40 p.m. Chepstow to Newport. In the years immediately before the Second World War, Severn Tunnel Jct. saw a diesel car from Pontypool Road and auto from Newport on the Wye Valley services. The Ebbw Jct. diesel car operations between Newport, Chepstow and Monmouth started in 1940.

A pair of 'Halls' – Bath Road's No.4983 *Albert Hall* and Canton's 6939 *Calveley Hall* – preparing to move across from the Down Tunnel line to the Down Main with the 7.30 a.m. Penzance (2.5 p.m. Bristol) to Manchester on Thursday, 27th June 1957. The service also conveyed through coaches from Kingswear to Liverpool and Birkenhead, and a restaurant car between Plymouth and Manchester. The Canton 'Hall' was working Turn 14 (designated for a 'Britannia') which started the day on the 1.15 a.m. Cardiff to Swansea (6.50 p.m. Swindon parcels), then the 6.45 a.m. Swansea to Bristol (Weston-super-Mare train), the 7.5 a.m. Penzance from Bristol to Pontypool Road, and finally the 4.45 p.m, Pontypool Road to Cardiff At Pontypool Road, the 'Halls' would hand over the Manchester-bound train to a Longsight 'Jubilee', 'Patriot' or 'Royal Scot' for the final part of the journey.

and loops were approved, as was an avoiding line to 'Benacre Bridge'. The junction between the Tunnel and Gloucester lines was improved in 1906/7, and avoiding lines to Undy Crossing provided in 1911. The pressure of the Great War caused additional goods lines and sidings to be built in 1916, and again in 1918. By 1920, the marshalling facilities comprised the Bristol Yard and West Sidings on the Up side, and the Down yard on the south side of the running lines; these gave a dozen or so sidings on each side, with goods running and reception lines in addition. All sidings were dead-end. As part of the Government scheme of 1929, the Bristol Yard was augmented and converted into loop accommodation in 1930/31. The yards could now hold 2,900 wagons. The next major development in the yards occurred in 1938/9, when the New Bristol Up yard was converted into a hump yard, whilst the Down was adapted into loops and similarly converted to a hump.

'Castle' No.5039 *Rhuddlan Castle* passing over onto the tunnel line at the west end of the station with train No.740, the 11.10 a.m. Milford Haven to Paddington, on Saturday, 21st March 1953; this engine was stationed at Carmarthen, transferred from Old Oak to that shed along with No.5043 in June 1952, renewing the 'Castle' allocation there. The bridge at the west end of the platform carried the small road from Roggiett onto the moors adjoining the River Severn. The station nameboard on the tunnel line platform informed passengers bound for Chepstow, the Monmouth line, and Lydney to change here, but those on the other platforms merely gave the station name.

Train No.208, the 9.5 a.m. Liverpool to Plymouth, passing through No.1 platform on Thursday, 27th June 1957 behind No.5078 *Beaufort*. The engine was from Newton Abbot shed, and worked a double-home turn involving the 8.0 a.m. Plymouth to Manchester train from Newton to Shrewsbury on Mondays, Wednesdays and Fridays, returning with the 9.10 a.m. Liverpool, 11.18 a.m. from Shrewsbury to Newton on Tuesdays, Thursdays, and Saturdays (11.47 a.m.). The formation of this train incorporated the main portion (including a dining car) to Plymouth with a small section for Paignton. Low-mileage 'Castles' and 'Counties' were used, and Newton also employed their 'Britannia' No.70022 *Tornado* until it was transferred to Canton in January 1957. A carriage truck for the car train through the tunnel can be seen to the right of the engine.

Ten Standard Class '4' 4–6–0s (75000–09) were introduced onto the Western Region at Shrewsbury in the latter part of 1951. Between September and November 1953, Nos.75007, 75008 and 75009 were transferred to Canton, along with 75021 and 75022, new from Swindon works, and were a familiar sight through Severn Tunnel Jct. thereafter. This view shows No.75021 from Canton shed approaching the station on the Gloucester road with the 1.50 p.m. Cardiff to Cheltenham on 27th June 1957. All of the '75XXX' engines were transferred away from South Wales in 1958.

The 2.5 p.m. Cardiff to Bristol local crossing onto the Tunnel line at the west end of the station behind Canton 'Hall' No.6969 *Wraysbury Hall* on 27th June 1957. The train comprised a remarkable selection of vehicles, including a 70ft 'Toplight' Van Second, a 60ft 'Centenary' Second, with a scheduled Compo, Second and Van Second behind; the 'Second' designation in place of 'Third' was introduced in 1956. The 1935 'Centenary' vehicles were subject to a number of route restrictions, which, in South Wales, included the main-line section between Newport (Maindee Jct.) and Little Mill Jct. (Pontypool Road). The turn being worked by the engine was a three-day diagram, utilising three Canton locomotives, which involved a Cardiff to Salisbury sequence on one day, a Salisbury, Bristol, Salisbury and Cardiff the next, with a Cardiff, Gloucester, Swindon and Cardiff on the final day; a different set of services were worked on Saturdays and Sundays when the turn incorporated either of those days.

Severn Tunnel Jct. had by now become the largest and most important marshalling yard on the GWR, being the focal point for a very large percentage of the traffic from and to South Wales, the company's principal freight-originating area, mostly of class 1 coal traffic. In the late 1930s, the South Wales and Monmouthshire collieries produced around 35 million tons of coal annually, of which about half went to the docks for shipment, whilst much of the balance was sent out to England via Severn Tunnel Jct. or Pontypool Road. In the down direction, large numbers of empty mineral wagons were returned to South Wales collieries, balancing the number of loaded vehicles sent into England, and also to meet upsurges in demand beyond the capability of South Wales to meet from its own resources. In this respect, the pooling of private owner vehicles during war years proved highly beneficial, and vastly reduced the amount of empties conveyed and the level of shunting required.

From around 1910, much of the locomotive coal was conveyed in 20-tonners, and often bypassed the Severn Tunnel Jct. yards in through trains from Aberdare or Rogerstone to London, the South and the West of England. Iron and steel production in South Wales and Monmouthshire during the late 1930s was second only to the North-East of England; next to the coal trade, it was the most important industry in South Wales, with around 3 million tons conveyed by the Great Western in 1938, mostly in the South Wales area. Other principal traffics passing through Severn Tunnel Jct. at that time included building materials, gravel, sand, cement, lime, iron ore, packed manure, grain, oil cake, timber, and road-making materials in full load quantities, as well as many vans of goods sundries.

The overall traffic pattern continued and expanded through the war, but eased gradually into the 1960s, latterly with a great reduction in coal traffic. Exceptions to the latter were smokeless fuels, and South Wales held a strong hand in this traffic with Phurnacite from Abercwmboi (Mountain Ash), and anthracite from the Neath, Swansea and Llanelly areas, together with smokeless coals from the Aberdare district; much of this passed through Severn Tunnel Jct. yards.

A progressive closure of branch lines and intermediate stations meant that the bay platforms became redundant, and by the late 1960s the through platform faces sufficed at Severn Tunnel Jct.

The high number of empty mineral wagons being sent into South Wales, together with insufficient clearance services, caused the working of the Down Yard to become inefficient, and when the operation of South Wales yards was replanned in 1970, alternative measures were effected. An empty mineral concentration yard was set up at Newport, East Usk, to handle incoming wagons from England, and the out-turn from Llanwern and Uskmouth power station. The disengagement firstly from goods shed traffic in 1972, and then from wagon-load traffic in 1976 had a heavy effect on the throughput of, and thus the need for, the huge yards at Severn Tunnel Jct. Facilities were therefore gradually reduced, and meaningful freight activity ceased during the 1980s, thus ending the era of the marshalling yard as a major part of the railway scene in the area.

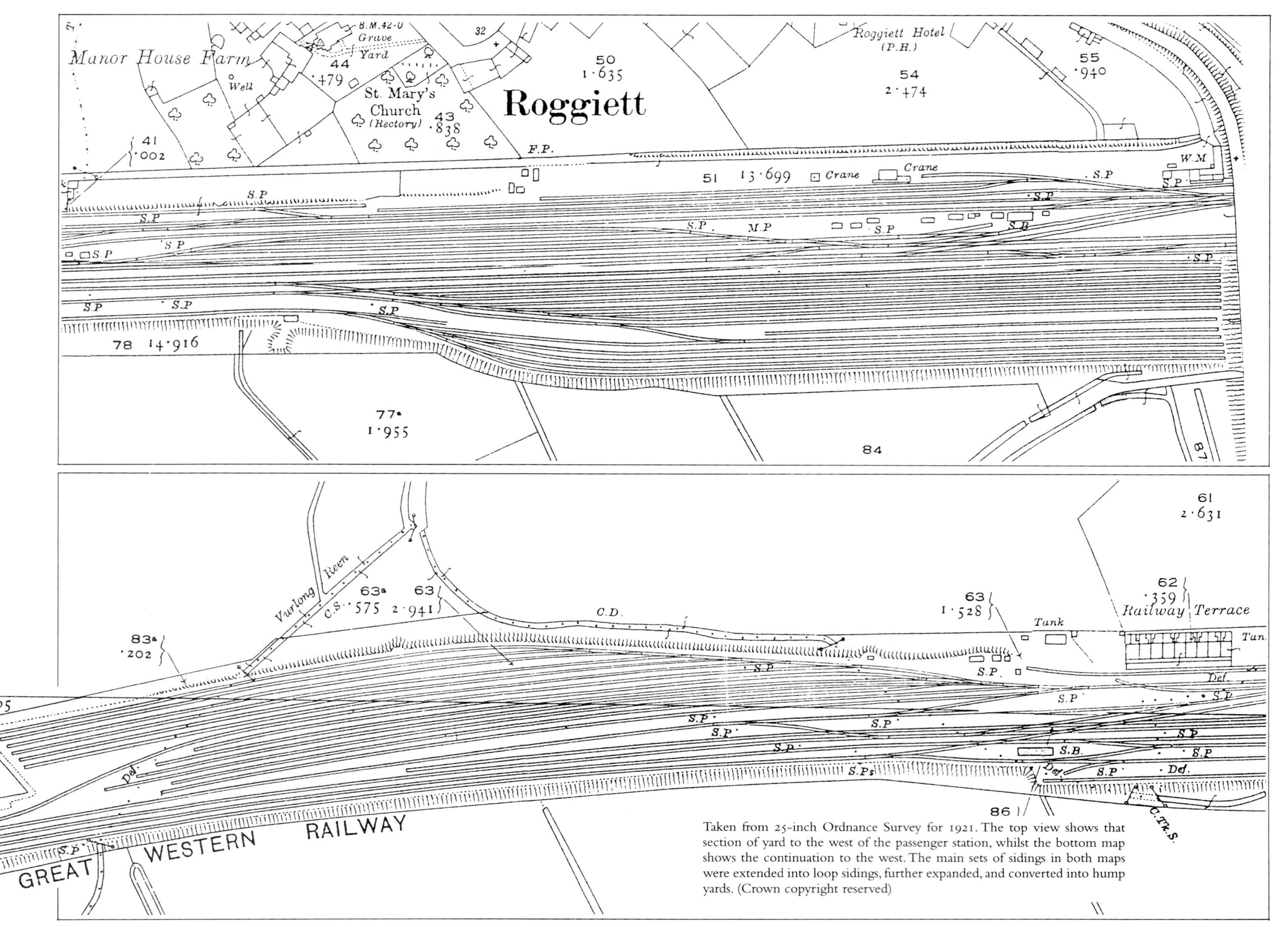

Taken from 25-inch Ordnance Survey for 1921. The top view shows that section of yard to the west of the passenger station, whilst the bottom map shows the continuation to the west. The main sets of sidings in both maps were extended into loop sidings, further expanded, and converted into hump yards. (Crown copyright reserved)

'61XX' No.6119 assisting Canton '28XX' No.3817 along the Up Goods Relief line behind Middle box (a westwards 'extension' of the Tunnel line) with an early afternoon freight, having emerged from the up yard further to the west, on 27th June 1957. In GWR days, the '61s' were contained entirely within the London Division (apart from temporary allocation to the West Country during the war), but a few moved to Bath Road shed in 1950/1. Newport Ebbw Jct. received an allocation in 1952/3, and Severn Tunnel Jct. in 1956, Nos.6119 and 6155 forming the initial allocation at the latter shed. With the onset of dieselisation in the London Division during the early 1960s, more of these engines became available for work elsewhere; nevertheless, two-thirds of the class were still in the London area in late 1961.

'3150' class 2–6–2T No.3172 at the west end of the station, with the 'T7' banker target displayed. The engine was just off shed, and was backing down towards the up yard for a spell of duty on Thursday, 27th June 1957. The target 'T7' engine came off shed at 2.30 p.m. for a 16-hour duty from Tuesdays to Saturdays inclusive, 9½ hours on Mondays and 3½ on Sundays. The 2–6–2Ts were first allocated to the depot around the turn of the year 1907/8 for banking duties, when two new engines (Nos.3177 and 3178) replaced some '1854' class 0–6–0 tanks, which in turn had taken over from '2721' class locomotives. The change was clearly a success, and by 1913 there were six '3100' class with a few '1854s'; by 1916, there were nine '3100s' and three '3150s'. This allocation grew to eight '3100s' and seven '3150s' by 1920, after which the emphasis moved to the latter series, with sixteen '3150s' by 1934. Thereafter, a gradual reduction in numbers occurred until the last examples went in 1958. No.3172 was withdrawn in October 1957.

On Saturday, 14th May 1960, Canton 'Castle' No.5099 *Compton Castle* passing Middle box on the Up Main with the up 'Red Dragon' (7.30 a.m. Carmarthen). The down (left) and up (right) marshalling yards are clearly visible to the west, each equipped with a hump. According to the Canton shedmaster, No.5099 was the finest 'Castle' to pass into his hands. A good 'Castle' would still join 'Britannias' on the Top Link of London trains at this time.

No.4079 *Pendennis Castle* passing Severn Tunnel Jct. Middle box on 26th April 1964 with a Birmingham to Swindon (via North & West route) SLS special, taking the Gloucester line through the station. This picture affords an excellent view of the Down marshalling yard on the left, which comprised down goods and reception loops/sidings nearest the running lines, 19 loop sidings of the hump itself, and another seven loops and sidings beyond, on the south edge of the yard.

The west end of the Severn Tunnel Jct complex, with Severn Tunnel shed's '2800' class No.2861 on the Down Relief with a class 'F' train of empties on 14th May 1960 – I photographed this train a couple of hours earlier as it climbed out of the tunnel. The new up reception sidings are seen on the left, with the disused Undy Crossing box in the distance; at one time, there were seven level crossings between Severn Tunnel Jct. and Newport. Although steel mineral wagons predominated by this time, a few timber-built vehicles may still be seen in the two trains in view. This view was taken from the eastern over-bridge at Undy.

'Britannia' No. 70018 *Flying Dutchman* passing over the troughs with the down 'South Wales Pullman' on 26th July 1956.

Undy ('Magor') troughs served the two main lines only. This view shows Newton Abbot 'Castle' No.5024 *Carew Castle* taking water on Saturday, 14th May 1960, while working the 9.5 a.m. Liverpool to Plymouth service. Each trough was 560 yards in length. In the event of Magor troughs being unserviceable, down London express trains had to take a full tank at Newport or Cardiff as required, having used Sodbury beforehand. Up London trains were to take a full tank at Cardiff to take them the forty miles through to Sodbury. North & West services were to pick up at Bristol, Hereford and Pontypool Road. The trough tank is seen on the left, with the Little Hill footbridge beyond; the divergence around the tank by the 1941 extension of the goods lines from Magor to Undy Crossing is clearly evident, with the cutting widened to accommodate the Down Relief, and the footbridge extended.

No.3714 from Ebbw Jct. shed, running over Magor troughs with a Newport to Chepstow local on 14th May 1960. Apart from ex-ROD and constituents, all tenders were fitted with water pick-up apparatus, although tank engines by this time were not. The 4–4–2 'County Tanks' were originally fitted with the apparatus to enable some long scheduled runs, as were the '36XX' 2–4–2Ts and some early '31XX' 2–6–2Ts, although it had been removed from the tank classes by the early 1920s.

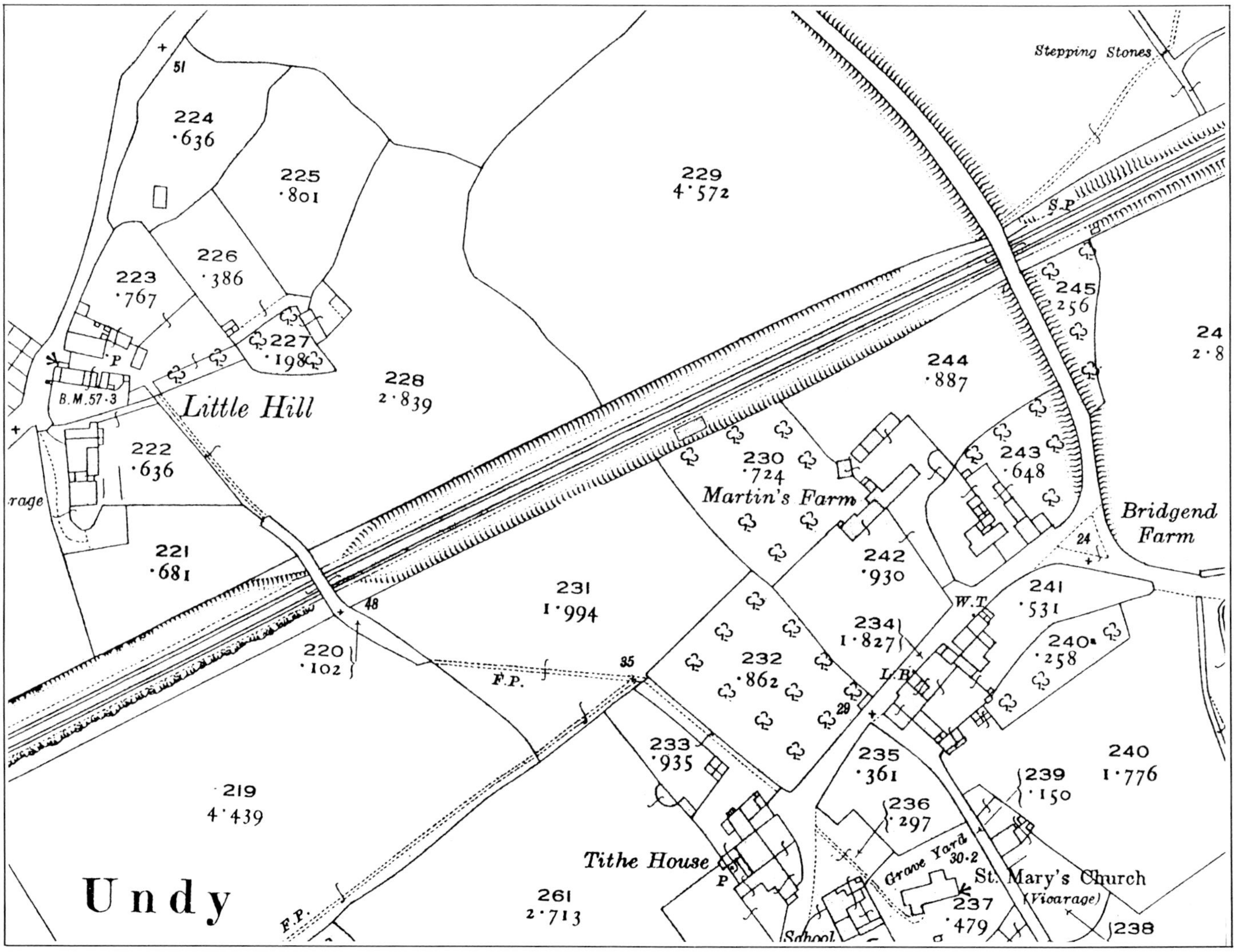

Stepping Stones
Little Hill
Martin's Farm
Bridgend Farm
Tithe House
St. Mary's Church
(Vicarage)
Grave Yard
School
Undy

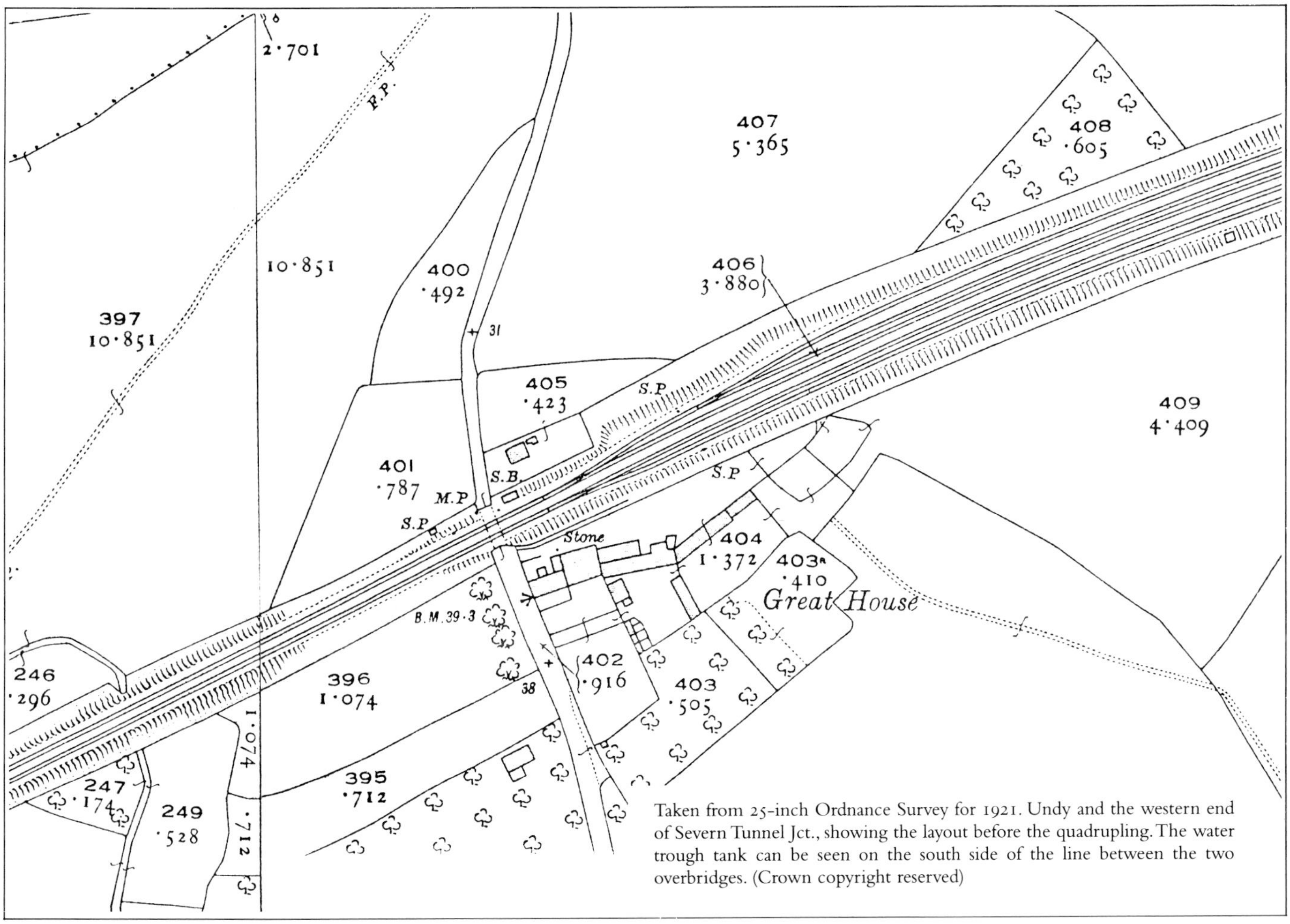

Taken from 25-inch Ordnance Survey for 1921. Undy and the western end of Severn Tunnel Jct., showing the layout before the quadrupling. The water trough tank can be seen on the south side of the line between the two overbridges. (Crown copyright reserved)

This view on the east side of the road bridge shows Severn Tunnel 'Hall' No.6905 *Claughton Hall* running along the Up Relief line at the western end of the Severn Tunnel Jct. complex. The engine was paired with an 8-wheeled tender No.2586, built in July 1931, and the only GWR example of the genre apart from the 'double-bogie' version built for the *Great Bear* (withdrawn in 1936). Other 'Halls' to carry this tender included Nos.5919 (1931), 4918 (1950/1), Nos.6951 (1956/7) and 5904(1961–3). The new, and as yet incomplete, reception roads for the up hump yard can be seen beyond the engine. Four reception roads were originally sandwiched between the running lines and the hump yard, but the new location allowed eleven to be provided on the approach, with additional dead-end storage sidings available to the north of the hump, which retained its 21 roads. 14th May 1960.

'9F' 2–10–0 No.92215 passing through Undy Halt with an up class 'H' mineral on 14th May 1960. The westernmost part of Undy village is in the background, with Magor not far beyond. Magor station was a half-mile further down the line. There are still a fair number of wooden wagons on the train, with some 21-tonners further back.

FROM UNDY TO THE USK

Old Oak 'Castle' No.4082 *Windsor Castle* with train 719, the 11.55 am. Paddington to Pembroke Dock, running towards Undy Halt. The rear part of the train was still over Magor troughs as it passed under Little Hill footbridge and cleared the western extremity of Severn Tunnel Jct. complex. The cutting here was widened considerably in the wartime works, in which the Up and Down Relief lines were added to the centrally-placed Mains. The photograph was taken from the western overbridge at Undy.

The seven-mile section of line between Severn Tunnel Jct. and the eastern outskirts of Newport followed the northern bank of the Severn Estuary, running about a mile inland over fairly flat ground. With the opening of the line in June 1850, intermediate stations to the west of Portskewett were initially provided at Magor and Llanwern.

UNDY TO LLANWERN

Magor became a useful terminal to serve the local farming area, with three yard sidings including a cattle pen by 1920, by when a long refuge siding had also been provided on both the up and down side. In the 1941 quadrupling of the line between Severn Tunnel and Newport, these became the new Up and Down Goods lines. Though the station was closed to passengers in November 1964, the yard remained open and was principally used to handle cement trains from Hoo Jct. in connection with the construction of the M4 Motorway, this traffic lasting until mid-1965, when the yard was closed.

The original layout through Bishton was up and down lines only, with a level crossing and signal box opened in 1908. In 1920, new up and down loops were introduced, controlled at the east end by Bishton East Signal Box with the level crossing box at the west end renamed Bishton West, both boxes being on the down side. The 1941 quadrupling of the running lines stopped short in both directions at the Bishton level crossing and enabled Bishton East box to be closed, while the West box was moved to the up side. The 1961 alterations in connection with the building of Llanwern Steelworks saw the eastern access lines to the plant go off just beyond Bishton level crossing. The previous crossings between the up and down lines were taken out, enabling the signal box to be reduced to a ground frame. Some 60 chains from the Llanwern eastern access, a new flyover was constructed to carry the up relief line over to the north side of the up main in order to provide access into Severn Tunnel Marshalling Yard, the track configuration reverting to its former order of Up Relief, Up Main, Down Main, Down Relief, which had proved so problematical west of Llanwern.

Llanwern was originally double track serving an up and down platform, but probably by the new century, a level crossing had been installed with a goods shed and loading dock, together with an up refuge siding, soon to be expanded into an up goods loop, and also a down refuge siding. On the up side of the line, Llanwern Lime Works had long leads into both the up and down lines at the west end and into the up line at the east end, but these were removed in 1927. In the quadrupling of the line in 1941, the lines through Llanwern station originally remained double only, the four-track formation ending just east of the platforms and restarting just beyond the level crossing at the west. Later in the year, the up and down goods lines were joined, running behind the up and down platforms. The station and goods yard were closed in September 1960, and under the 1961 alterations to layout, the level crossing and platforms were removed and four plain lengths of track ran where this once-cherished local station had stood.

The only change was the opening of Undy Halt, a half-mile to the east of Magor station, on 11th September 1933, bringing the number of intermediate stations on the line between Severn Tunnel Jct. and Newport to three.

UNDY HALT

'64XX' 0-6-0PT No.6408 at Undy Halt with an empty 'B' set, 30th July 1960, working to Chepstow, for Monmouth. The 'C' class headlamp was used for empty coaching stock not specially authorised to carry an 'A' lamp. The halt was opened for traffic in September 1933, and in the post-1941 layout served only the main lines, with the footbridge connecting the platforms with both parts of the village. The halt was closed in November 1964. This view was taken looking westwards from the west Undy overbridge.

Canton 'Britannia' No.70016 *Ariel* on the 8.0 a.m. Neyland to Paddington ('A58') at Undy Halt, 30th July 1960. This was the year (as from 13th June) in which the new four-character train identification system came into force for express services. On steam-hauled services, a letter and two numbers replaced the original three numerals, whilst the class of the train was still indicated by the headlamps; diesels used a number prefix ('1' for a class 'A' train, for example) to the reporting number. The intention to identify every 'A' (or class '1') passenger train was earmarked for introduction in the summer of 1959, but the shortfall in the 250 additional frames and 1,500 number plates required for the steam locomotives caused a year's delay. Once more, an ex-LNER coach is seen at the head of the formation for strengthening.

Tyseley 'Hall' No.6904 *Charfield Hall* passing through Undy Halt with a down express on Tuesday, 26th June 1956. The train is probably the 8.50 a.m. Birmingham to Cardiff, running via Gloucester, which was worked through by a Tyseley engine; both engine and stock were scheduled to return as the 5.10 p.m. Cardiff to Birmingham that evening. The western overbridge at Undy is shown in the background.

Ebbw Jct. '28XX' class 2–8–0 No.3807 approaching Undy Halt with an up freight on 26th June 1956. At this time, the '28s' were still the most numerous heavy goods engines seen in this part of South Wales, with over 80 shared between Severn Tunnel Jct., Ebbw Jct., Aberdare and Canton, half of which were at Severn Tunnel. 'Austerities' were also present, with 17 at Ebbw Jct. and Canton, mostly the latter. The road on the right is the B4245, which took the scenic loop off the A48 Chepstow to Newport trunk route, with Magor village in the distance, and its station a short distance around the bend.

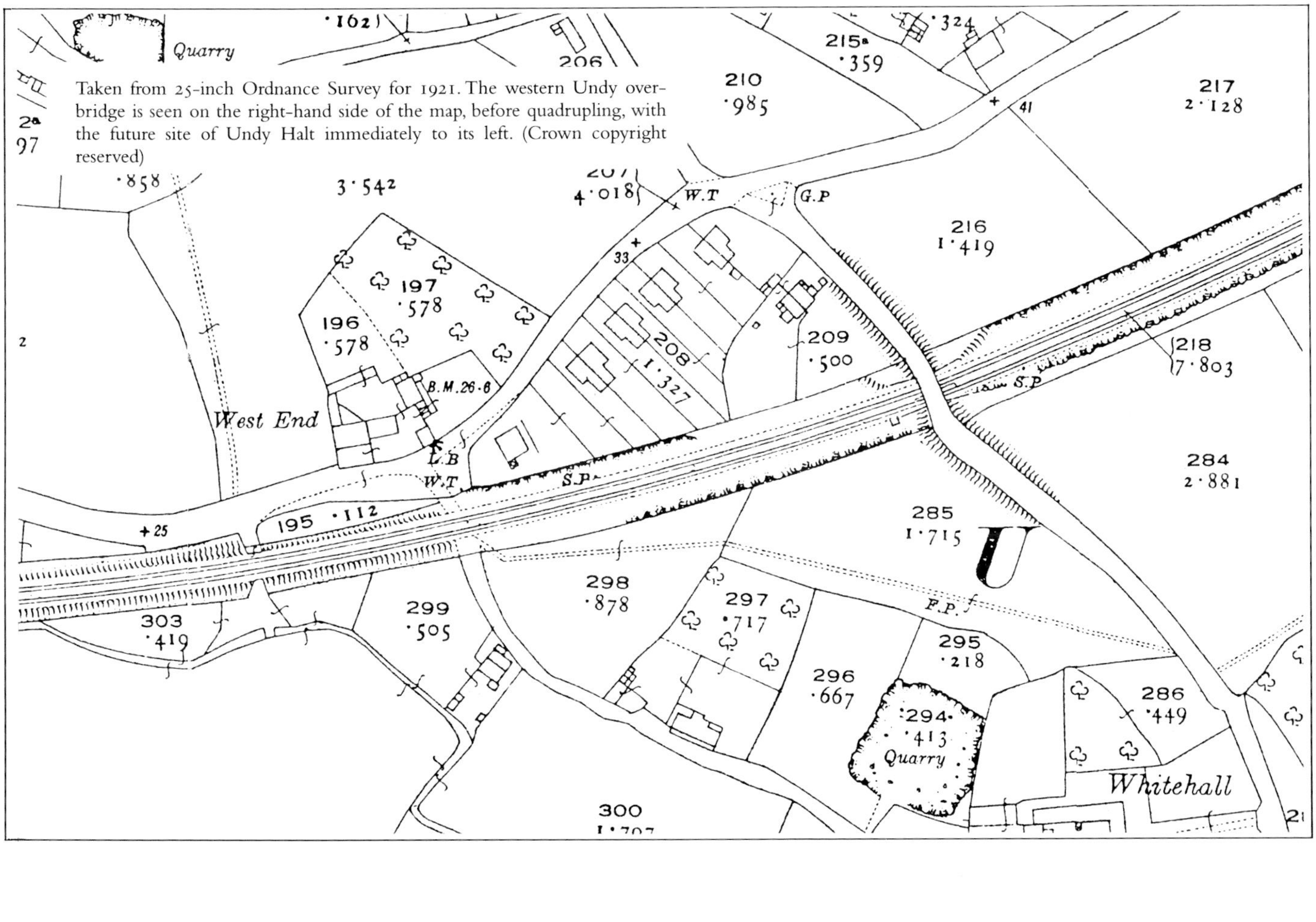

Taken from 25-inch Ordnance Survey for 1921. The western Undy over-bridge is seen on the right-hand side of the map, before quadrupling, with the future site of Undy Halt immediately to its left. (Crown copyright reserved)

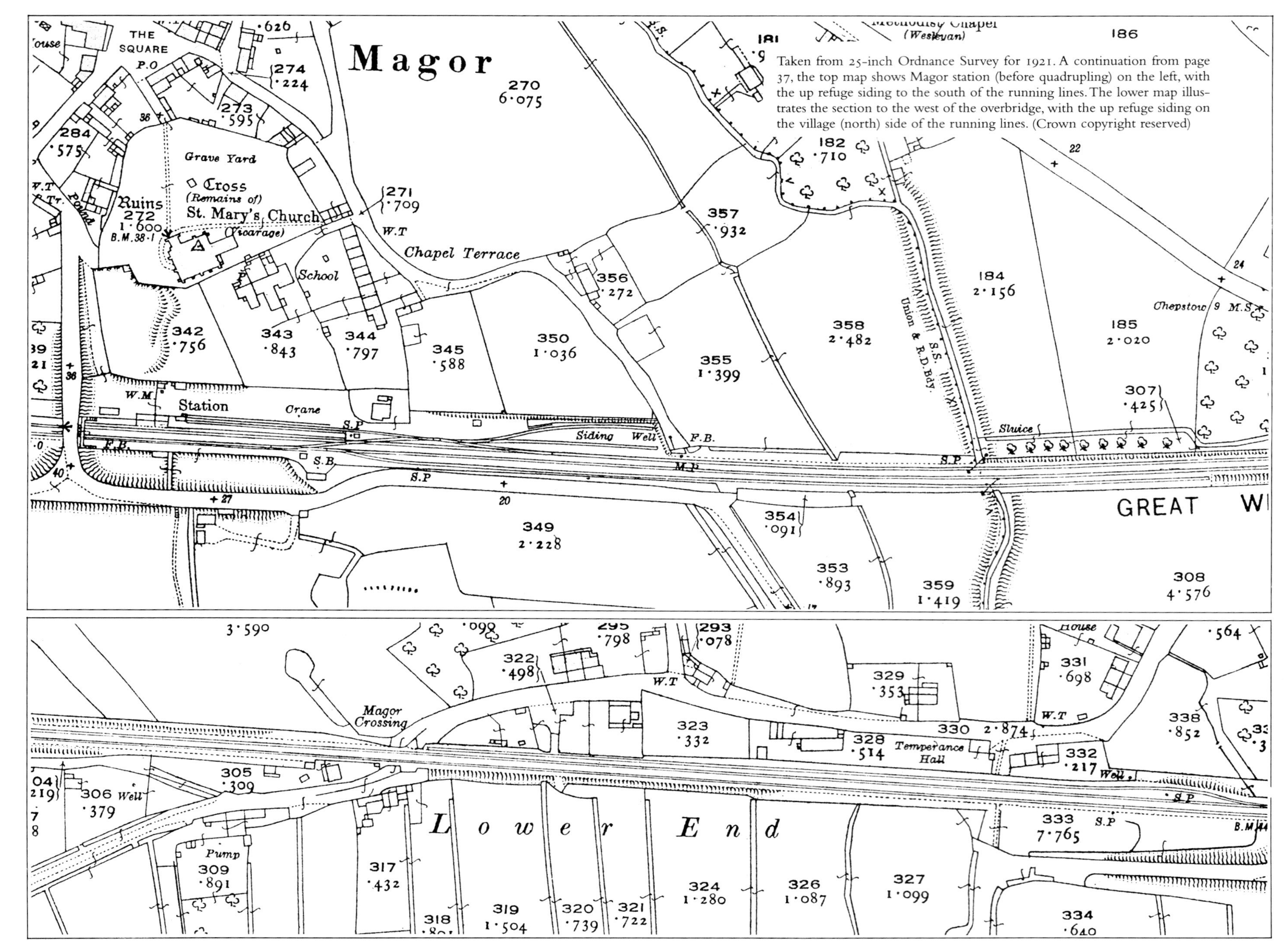

Taken from 25-inch Ordnance Survey for 1921. A continuation from page 37, the top map shows Magor station (before quadrupling) on the left, with the up refuge siding to the south of the running lines. The lower map illustrates the section to the west of the overbridge, with the up refuge siding on the village (north) side of the running lines. (Crown copyright reserved)

MAGOR

Westbury 'Hall' No.4930 *Hagley Hall* passing through Magor station with an up Bristol fast on 26th June 1956. Magor station comprised two 'island' platforms, serving, like Undy Halt, the two main lines to the centre only, and connected to the outside world by a footbridge. Outside the platforms ran the two goods loops, installed in late 1941. The small goods yard is seen to the right of the train, with Magor village beyond.

'Britannia' No.70022 *Tornado*, from Newton Abbot shed, is seen here with the 9.10 a.m. Liverpool to Plymouth service (Train No.247) on the Up Main at Bishton on Thursday, 19th November 1953, working the double-home turn from Shrewsbury. Bishton box and level crossing were a little further to the right of the picture, together with several crossovers connecting the four running lines. Unlike Undy, Bishton was not provided with a halt, and would-be passengers would have to make their way to the station at Llanwern, some two miles away across the fields.

A Gloucester WD 'Austerity' 2–8–0 No.90524 with an up coal train at Bishton on 19th November 1953. The WDs were designed by Robin Riddles on a basic premise of a 1,000-ton load at 40 mph on level track, with a 15½ ton axle load permitting wide route availability. The first of these engines appeared on the Great Western in the autumn of 1944, though they had returned to the WD by early 1945. They returned to the system from late 1946, this time to remain until the final years of steam. The 'Austerities' were designated 'Blue' route colour, and the power group 'E', with a tender capacity of 9 tons of coal and 5,000 gallons of water.

Nearly all of Ebbw Jct.'s scheduled 'Grange' turns were freight, the one exception being a Newport, Gloucester, Swansea and Newport passenger diagram. No.6812 *Chesford Grange* with a class 'H' mineral on the Up Relief at Bishton on 19th November 1953. The engine was from Ebbw Jct. shed, and its load of coal therefore probably from the valleys above Newport.

LLANWERN

Llanwern station, looking eastwards on 9th June 1960, showing the two platforms with their basic shelters fenced off from the goods lines on either side. This picture shows Ebbw Jct's '9400' class 0–6–0PT No.9482 skirting the station with a down class 'K' freight. This engine was built in September 1952, and survived a mere eleven years in traffic – longer than some of its class – being withdrawn in November 1963.

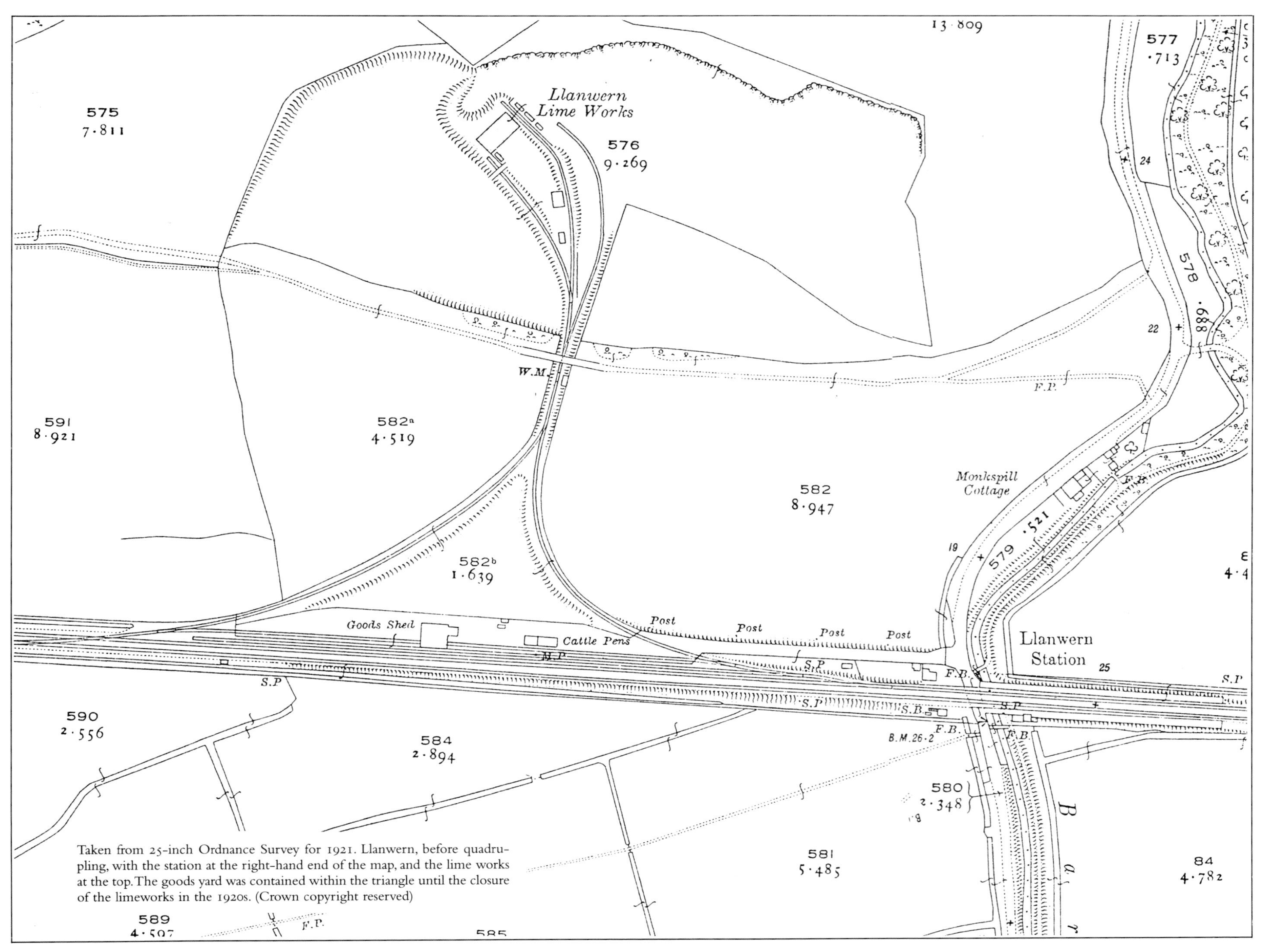

Taken from 25-inch Ordnance Survey for 1921. Llanwern, before quadrupling, with the station at the right-hand end of the map, and the lime works at the top. The goods yard was contained within the triangle until the closure of the limeworks in the 1920s. (Crown copyright reserved)

'Hall' No.6955 *Lydcott Hall* from Westbury shed bringing the 10.30 a.m. Cardiff to Portsmouth train through Llanwern station on 9th June 1960. Westbury engines regularly worked through trains between Salisbury and Cardiff during the 1950s. As with Magor and Undy, the station comprised two island platforms serving the central pair of lines, joined to the station approach by a footbridge. The road crossing the railway at this point ran from Llanwern village (on the left) to the Welsh Grounds, on the mouth of the Severn, with access controlled from the adjacent Llanwern box. On the right can be seen the station building, positioned on the station approach road.

EAST USK TO MAINDEE

The main developments within the section during the earlier years occurred in the East Usk area. On the eastern outskirts of Newport, in the Lliswerry area (about a mile east of High Street station) was the small but important yard of East Usk, which served two important branches: the Nettlefolds Branch, which originally served the River Usk wharves from the west end of the sidings, and the Uskmouth Branch, which ran from the east end of the yard. In 1900, East Usk Yard contained only three short stopblocked sidings on either side of the main lines, but by 1920 a full yard of seven loop sidings had been created to serve the expanding industrial concerns in the area. By 1940, this had been increased to twelve loop sidings, plus a direct lead into Standard Telephone and Cables, who forwarded a large number of open wagons containing cable reels until 1968, when their private siding agreement terminated. In 1970, East Usk Yard became used as the empty mineral wagon concentration point for South Wales, receiving from England those empties previously worked through Severn Tunnel Jct. Yard, and also the empty wagon out-turn from Llanwern and Uskmouth Power Station. Full wagon inspection and repair facilities were also concentrated there. This took great pressure off Severn Tunnel Yard, and brought far greater cohesion to empty wagon supply to collieries. Though this function has now ceased, part of the yard is still in position.

At the east end of the yard, and opposite the East Usk Jct. signal box, was Lliswerry Mileage Yard which, along with Newport Goods Yard, undertook the delivery of full load traffic. During the 1960s the Civil Engineer set up a track pre-assembly depot alongside the main line, just east of the East Usk Branch, but this had closed within ten years.

The East Usk Branch left the main line just east of East Usk Jct. signal box, and is still operative. The branch originally had its own signal box, East Usk Branch Jct., located at the commencement of the branch at the east end of Lliswerry Mileage Yard, but this box had been closed by 1928. The first main works on the branch was originally known as the British Mannesmann Tube Works, which opened in 1914. From c.1938 this became the Newport & South Wales Tube Works, later becoming Stewart & Lloyds Tube Works, their private siding agreement eventually terminating in 1974. A short distance away on the western side of the line was Lysaghts Steelworks, which became the BSC Orb Works from 1951. Further down the branch on the river side was the Mount Stuart Dry Dock Co.'s Channel Dry Dock, whose private siding agreement was from 1905–70. Directly opposite this installation was the massive Monsanto Chemical Works, who began forwarding from their private siding in 1947. Next came the British Aluminium Company's site who ceased forwarding by rail in 1980. At the end of the branch was the Uskmouth Power Station. During the late 1950s, this was expanded by the building of the Uskmouth 'B' station, taking coal from several collieries in East Wales. Though subsequently closed, the station has now been re-opened and is fed by MGR services.

The Nettlefolds Branch deviated at the Newport end of East Usk Yard – with its own signal box, Nettlefolds Branch Jct, until about 1920 – and served the old dock wharves along the River Usk, the main installation being Great Western Wharf, around which the Usk Chemical Works and the Basic Slag & Phosphate Co. had sidings in later years. The line split shortly before reaching GW Wharf and continued west along the bank of the Usk, where the Imperial Wagon Works, the small Newport Power Station and the original Clarence Wharf could be found. Until 1931, the branch had been leased by Happerfield & Willans from Guest, Keen & Nettlefolds and from then until 1973, the Great Western Wharf was leased to the Basic Slag & Phosphate Co. and the remainder to Newport Corporation.

Another significant project in hand at Newport before the Great War, to ease congestion, was the widening and lengthening of Chepstow Road bridge in the eastern part of the town. The goods running loops were extended over the bridge in 1920.

Between East Usk Yard and the Usk river viaduct lies the important Maindee Junction, a triangular junction where the line to Caerleon, Pontypool and Hereford, which, with the building of the Severn Tunnel, became the West to North route, deviates from the main line to West Wales. In 1880, the lines between the East Usk Wharf branch (later Nettlefolds) and Maindee East box were quadruple, but beyond the East box became double. The original Maindee Jct. North box was at the immediate intersection of the track from Maindee Jct. West, but in 1907 the North junction was set back 13 chains and the box resited, in order to accommodate a new up and down loop. By the turn of the century, Maindee Jct. East had become a critical point for congestion and a new up loop was added in 1904, followed by a new signal box in 1905, located on the other (north) side of the line. A new down loop was brought into use from East Jct. part of the way to West Jct. in 1920, as part of the project to widen and lengthen Chepstow Road bridge. The loop was further extended in 1927 as part of the major alterations undertaken at Newport at the end of that decade, when the lines were quadrupled across the river bridge and Maindee West Jct. box was closed.

In the 1961 alterations, the Down Loop between the east and west ends of the triangle became the Up Relief and a new Down Relief line was added to complete the four-track configuration of Up Main, Down Main, Up Relief, Down Relief from Cardiff Newtown West to Bishton. With the electrification of the LMR Birmingham area in the mid-1960s, the West & North services which had used the Maindee Triangle were rerouted to run via Gloucester and the LMR to Birmingham New Street, and the WR West & North route became severely downgraded.

Within the Maindee triangle, there were sidings from as early as 1880, which were probably for engineer's use as they were later defined, there being seven such sidings in 1954 accessed from the

Taken from 25-inch Ordnance Survey for 1937. East Usk Yard. The area below the sidings was later developed industrially; the Bilston Street factory here was eventually taken over by the Standard Telephones & Cables company. (Crown copyright reserved)

west end, as part of a fully-fledged civil engineer's depot. Following the 1981 alterations, these sidings were replaced by four sidings accessed from the north end of the triangle by a Ground Frame.

LATER DEVELOPMENTS

The last significant alteration under the GWR was the quadrupling between the western end of Severn Tunnel Jct. and the eastern end of Newport East Usk, which took place in 1941, due largely to the pressure of wartime traffic. The line between Severn Tunnel Jct. and Newport was double from the outset, and in order to provide refuge for goods trains on this busy section, up and down goods loops were provided at Severn Tunnel Jct. itself, Bishton (just west of Magor) and Newport East. However, the need for quadruple track on this section became acute, to reduce the level of delays to goods services, and to handle the increasing amount of traffic passing. Though the subject was first raised before the Great War, it was not until 1941 that the work was carried out, when the strategic importance of the South Wales Docks to the national war effort demanded that capacity be increased as a matter of great urgency. The section was already feeling the pressure of wartime traffic – particularly goods and 'government stores' – and regularly became saturated.

Work was put in hand with such exigency that quadrupling was completed throughout in a little more than nine months. The section between Bishton and Llanwern was completed in February/March 1941, between Llanwern and Lliswerry in August, Magor and Bishton in September, Lliswerry and East Usk in October, and the final section from Undy Crossing to Magor in November. The new goods lines were each placed outside their respective mains, though the station platform faces still served only the mains, and had fencing on their outer faces.

The section of line between Severn Tunnel Jct. and Newport was transformed by the building of the Richard Thomas & Baldwin's Spencer Steelworks near Llanwern in 1961. To permit the reception of large volumes of iron ore and coking coal, it was necessary to redesign the track layout from Alexandra Dock Jct. to Llanwern so that the relief lines were on the coastal side with the main lines on the inland side. To have perpetuated the original layout between Newport East and Llanwern of Up Relief, Up Main, Down Main, Down Relief would have meant iron ore and coal trains crossing both main lines to enter the Llanwern Works, producing unacceptable delay. The redesignation of layout was accompanied by complete re-signalling of the area with the installation of Multiple Aspect Signalling, all completed by the end of 1962, full details of which are provided in the section on Newport.

The complex had access points with the relief lines at both the east and west ends, and had up and down service lines running the length of the complex, nearest to and parallel with the main lines outside. Initially, iron ore entered the plant at both the east and west ends, home ore from Banbury, etc, at the east and imported (foreign) ore at the west, where all the coking coal was also received from the South Wales coalfield, the majority from the Western Valley pits. Much of this coal was former locomotive coal which the NCB now blended with other coals and treated to become prime coking coal.

Near to the west end of the site, there was a nest of 10 loop sidings parallel with the service roads, the two nearest the plant being reserved for home ore reception and departure. An internal signalbox controlled movements at the west end of these sidings. Further to the east there were nine double-ended exchange sidings where outwards traffic was handed back to the railways, and at the eastern extremity, a final set of eight sidings which funnelled into a line running to the rear of the plant. At various points, sets of sidings ran off the service lines or sidings into the plant itself, supplying the many functions of the steelworks.

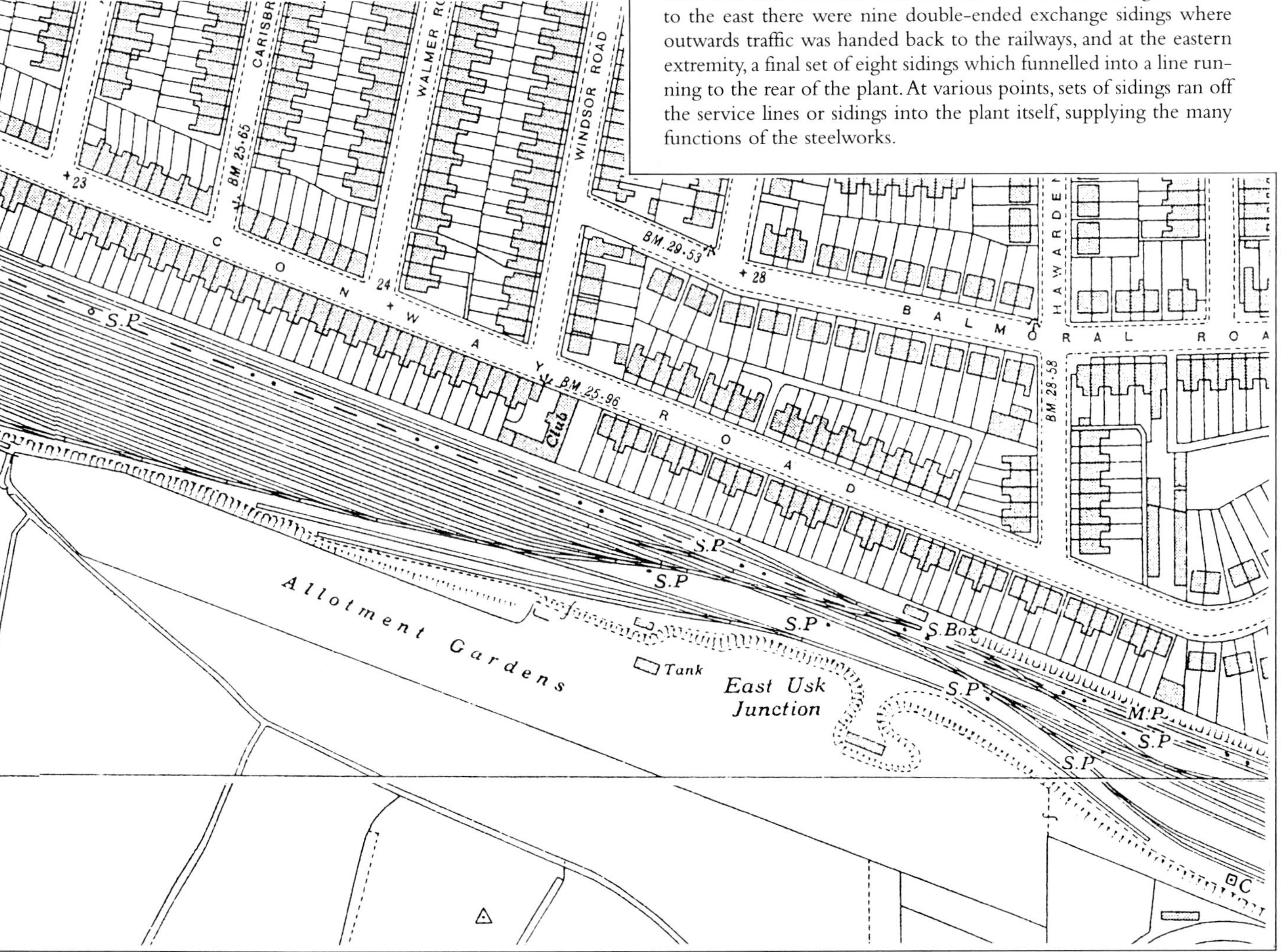

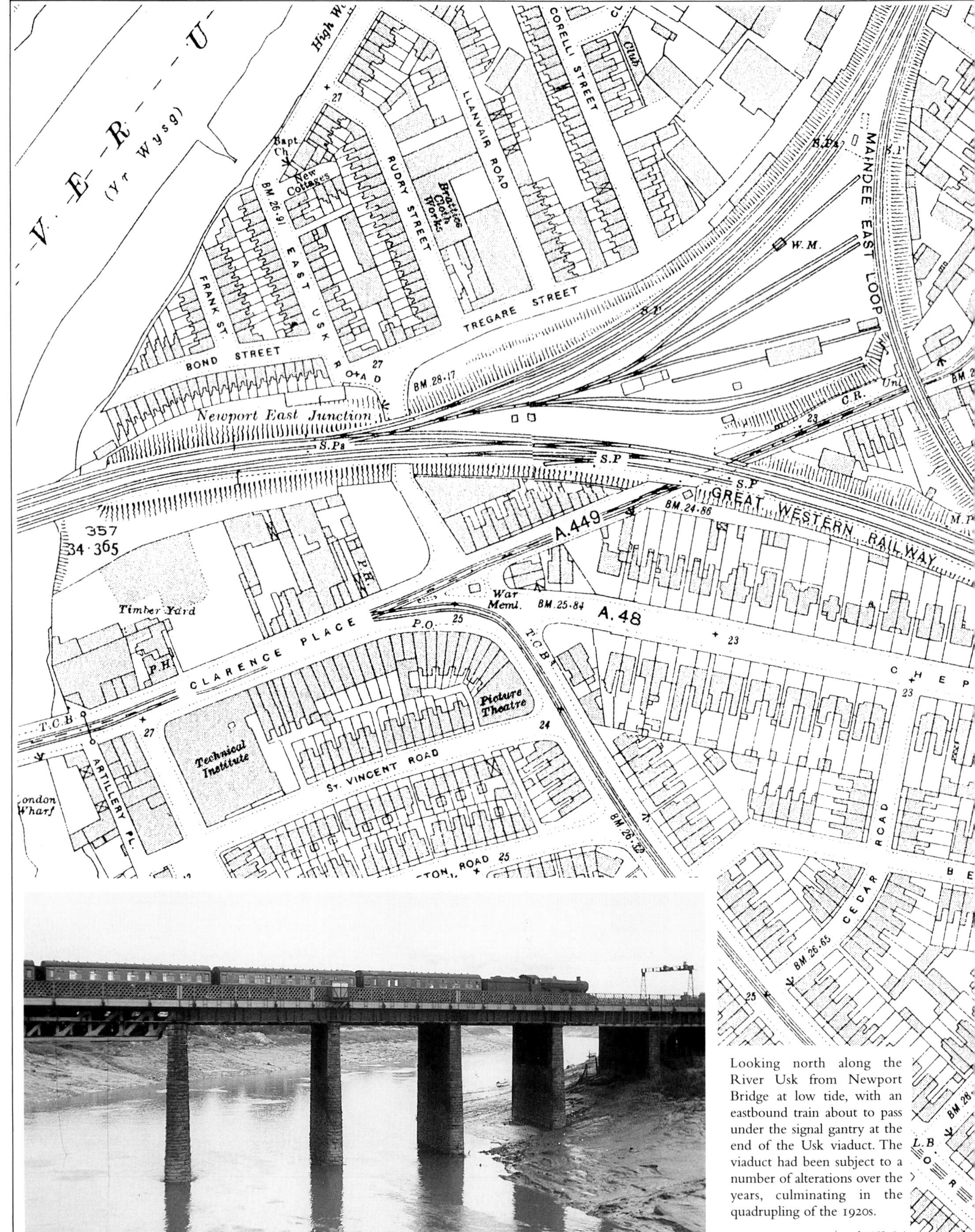

Looking north along the River Usk from Newport Bridge at low tide, with an eastbound train about to pass under the signal gantry at the end of the Usk viaduct. The viaduct had been subject to a number of alterations over the years, culminating in the quadrupling of the 1920s.

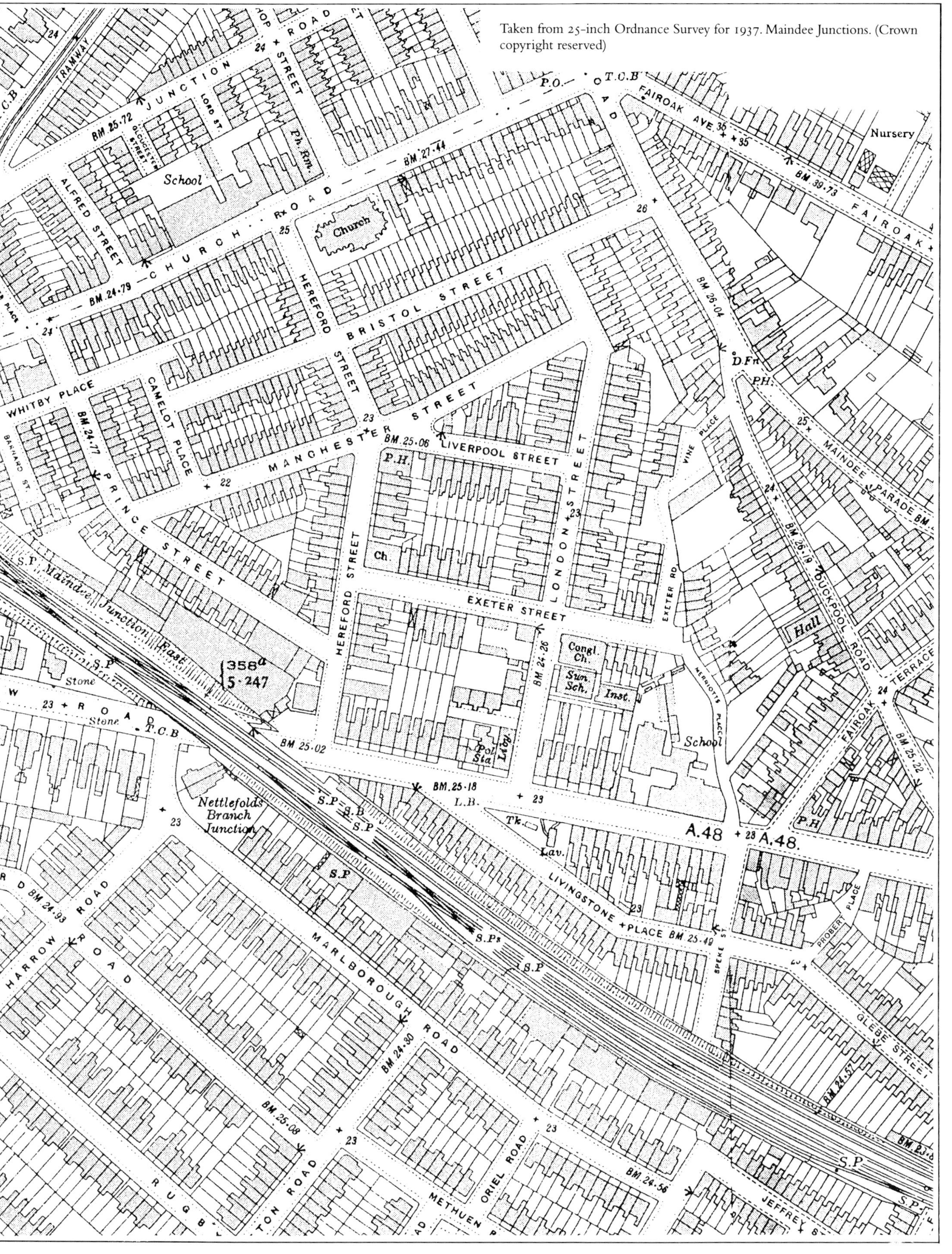

Taken from 25-inch Ordnance Survey for 1937. Maindee Junctions. (Crown copyright reserved)

NEWPORT HIGH STREET

ACROSS THE USK

In the process of entering Newport and continuing westwards to Cardiff and West Wales, Brunel was confronted with the crossing of the River Usk. The construction of the viaduct across the river was one of two major problems which faced the developers, the other being the Hillfield Tunnel. A viaduct of some 215 yards across the Usk was found necessary; this was built of timber with a central span of 100ft over the river, and designed for two broad-gauge tracks. It had been virtually completed when a workman securing a fixing with a red-hot bolt managed to set the timber alight. Being freshly kyanised, the timber structure went up in a blaze, and resort to the usual fire-extinguishing practices were abortive. Major reconstruction was necessary, and Brunel decided that the central span of the rebuilding should be of wrought iron; this was effected in the form of three bowstring girders side by side, with one track between each pair.

In 1888, the outer timber spans were replaced by wrought iron longitudinal girders, on the tops of which were laid the usual timber decks. New masonry piers were provided throughout.

During the years before the Great War, traffic had increased so much that it was considered necessary to provide four lines of way between Severn Tunnel Jct. and Newport. In connection with this, the Usk viaduct was to be widened, and extensions to the existing piers were constructed on the upstream side, starting in 1913. The demands of the Great War prevented a concerted effort to complete the project, though work on the piers continued slowly throughout the conflict. It was not until 1921 that the project was revived in earnest. New steelwork was built onto the 1913–19 pier extensions to carry the new up line, the old up line ironwork was replaced by steelwork, and the down line diverted onto it. The last of Brunel's bowstring girders were then removed, and the new steelwork completed on the seaward side to provide for the two further tracks. The new viaduct was of the decking type, with longitudinal girders from pier to pier, on top of which were laid 'Z' floor bearers, with plates riveted on to form the floor.

The former double track across the viaduct was quadrupled in 1927, thus removing a considerable bottleneck from the Newport area of the SWML.

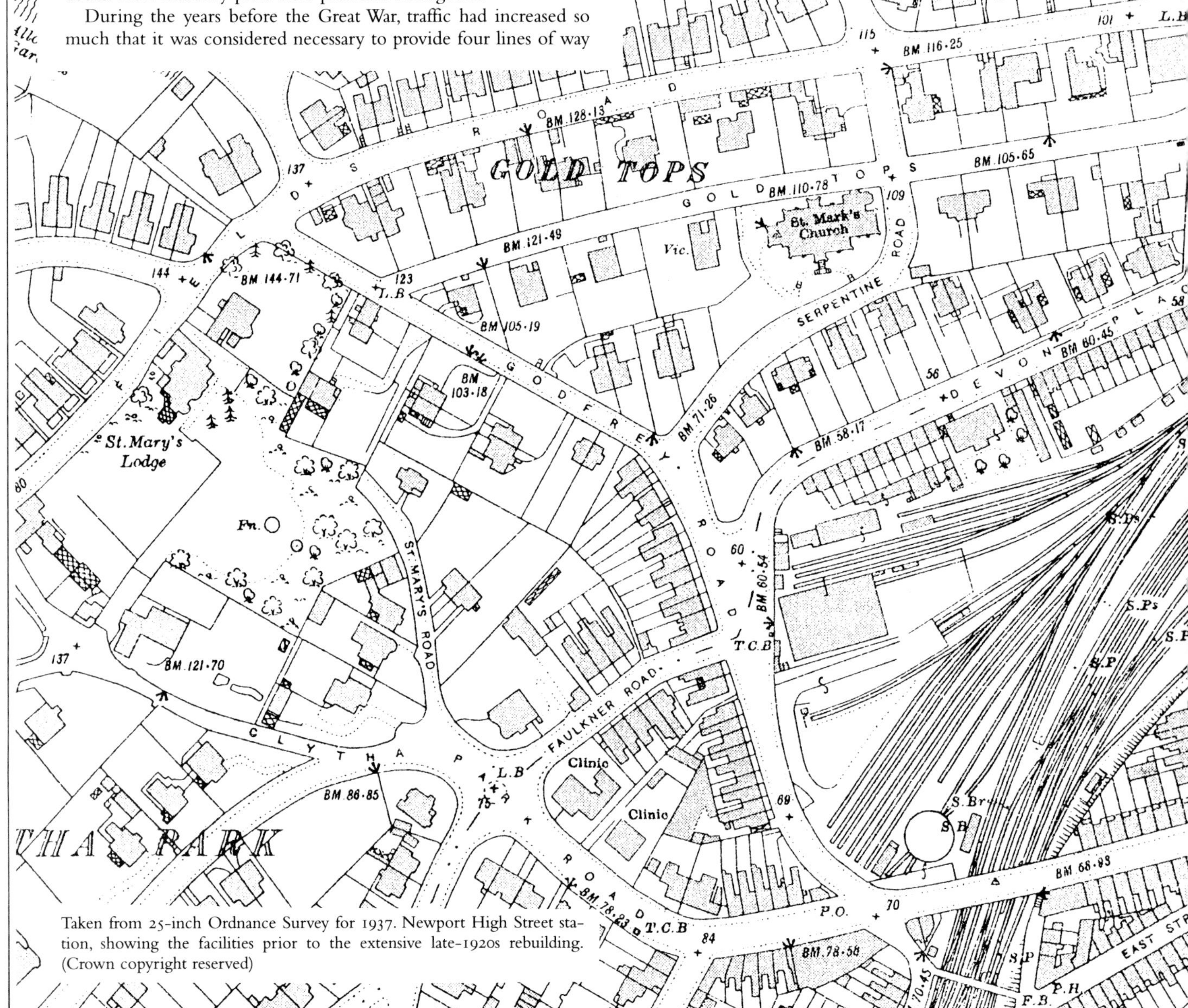

Taken from 25-inch Ordnance Survey for 1937. Newport High Street station, showing the facilities prior to the extensive late-1920s rebuilding. (Crown copyright reserved)

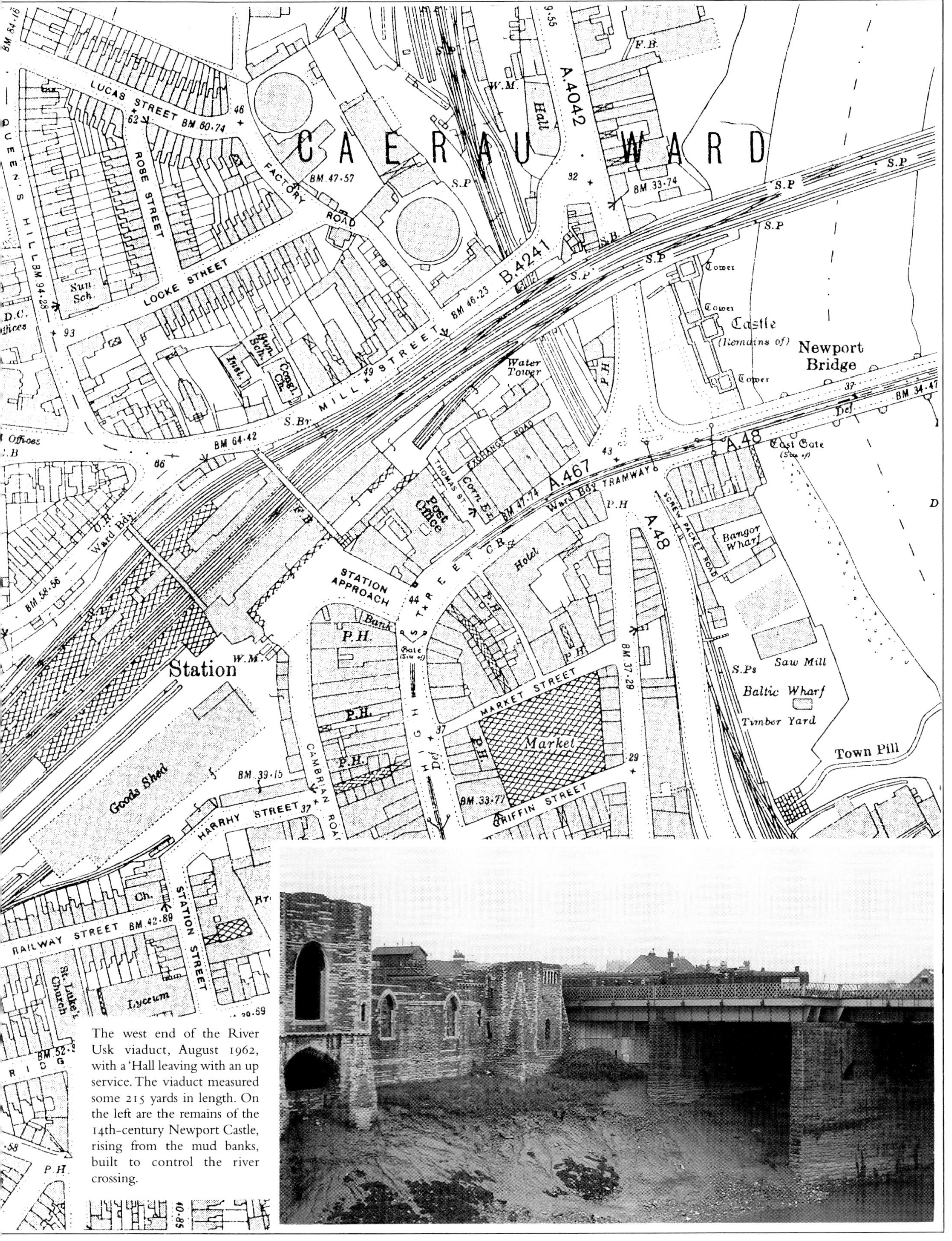

The west end of the River Usk viaduct, August 1962, with a 'Hall leaving with an up service. The viaduct measured some 215 yards in length. On the left are the remains of the 14th-century Newport Castle, rising from the mud banks, built to control the river crossing.

Old Oak 'Castle' No.4078 *Pembroke Castle* rolling off the Usk viaduct on the Down Main in the approach to High Street station with the 11.55 a.m. Paddington to Pembroke Dock service ('F23' carried, 'F32' designated) on 4th March 1961. During the winter months of the 1940s and 50s, this service was worked mostly by a Landore engine, but changes in the timetables would often bring Old Oak locomotives onto the scene, as was the case of 1953/54 and 1959/60. At this time, the train was worked to Cardiff by Old Oak men, who returned from there with the 4.0 p.m. (12.5 p.m. Milford Haven), with Canton men working on to Swansea.

HIGH STREET PASSENGER STATION

No.6693 from Pontypool Road shed running past Newport East box on the Down Main with a down local freight on 4th March 1961. Pontypool Road used their '56s' on both passenger and freight diagrams either across the Vale of Neath or to Newport or Cardiff, and also through to Barry Island during the summer with up to 10-coach excursions. Newport East box, located on the viaduct, was opened in 1927 to replace the old Newport East and Maindee West boxes in preparation for the imminent station rebuilding at High Street.

Newport High Street Passenger Station was located just to the west of the River Usk viaduct. Construction was placed in the hands of Hughes & Co. of Liverpool, who also built the first Cardiff and Swansea stations. The broad-gauge Newport station of 1850 comprised two main 200ft platforms, up and down, each served by a through track, with the main buildings on the down (south) side. A short bay and carriage spur with a vehicle turntable were provided at the east end of the down platform, giving direct access to the town. A level crossing was provided to cross Thomas Street over the railway at the east end of the station, though this was soon removed.

There was a connection from both running lines into the goods shed on the south side of the main lines, and on the up side, a siding ran from the east end of the up platform, around its rear and into the area north of the line, which by 1854 provided access to the engine shed (qv), fitting shop and carriage shed.

With the abandonment of the broad gauge in 1872, three standard-gauge lines were provided through the station. The up main line ran through the middle with a loop coming off at the west end to serve the up platform, rejoining the up main at the end of the up platform, while the down main line served the down platform. Connections at the west end, controlled by Newport Tunnel box, now provided access to and from the goods depot and yard.

With the amalgamation of the Monmouthshire Railway & Canal Co., which ran local Valley services, and the GWR in 1880, a link line was built (in 1879/80) between the Western Valley line and the main line, the junctions made being named Park Jct. and Gaer Jct. This enabled the Western & Sirhowy Valley trains to run into High Street, the passenger station at Dock Street then being closed, but remaining in use for goods traffic. Trains from the Eastern Valley also began running into High Street, enabling Mill Street also to be closed on the same basis.

In order to accommodate these trains at High Street, major reconstruction was necessary. Four tracks were now provided through the station, the two main lines running through the centre with loops off to serve both platforms which were considerably lengthened; the up platform was made into an island to cater for eastward departing trains emanating from the carriage sidings. This north face of the island platform was 825ft in length, with the south (up main) face 814ft. The down platform was extended to 897ft, with a west end bay of 428ft.

In order to increase flexibility of operation, two scissors crossovers were located between the through and the platform roads centrally on either side, thus dividing each platform into two. The down platform became Nos. 1 and 2, the down bay No.3, the south face of the up island platform Nos. 4 and 5, and the north face Nos. 6 and 7. Three signal boxes controlled movements throughout the station, Newport Tunnel box at the west end, a new Newport Centre box towards the west end of the island platform and Newport East between the east end of the station and the viaduct.

Main-line trains from London, Bristol, Gloucester and Hereford and also local services from the Eastern Valleys arrived at the down platform No.1/2. The down bay platform No.3 was used for departing services to the Western (GWR) and Sirhowy (L&NWR) valleys, and for Brecon & Merthyr services to Caerphilly, Pontypridd,

'14XX' 0–4–2T No.1421 hauling the two trailers forming the 11.50 a.m. Monmouth (Troy) to Newport service off the Usk viaduct on Saturday, 10th May 1958. This unit worked two Newport & Monmouth return trips each day, with another three from Severn Tunnel Jct. or Chepstow to Monmouth. Auto-train services from Newport to Monmouth are believed to have started in 1927, replacing trains of elderly conventional stock. After the closure of the Wye Valley line to Monmouth in January 1959, five daily auto services from Newport or Severn Tunnel Jct terminated at Chepstow instead. The two trailers scheduled for this service illustrate the compartment and saloon types.

'56XX' 0–6–2T No.6672 running past East box with a Blaenavon to Newport (Eastern Valley) passenger on 27th June 1953 comprising an elderly 'absorbed' coach, a corridor vehicle and a 'B' set. The train was heading for No.6 platform on the Down Relief line.

An Eastern Valleys service from Pontypool (Crane Street) approaching High Street station behind Pontypool Road '57XX' 0–6–0PT No.3703 on 14th September 1957. Engines from Ebbw Jct. and Pontypool Road operated the Eastern Valley passenger services. When the need for van space was minimal on three-coach trains, a single van third vehicle would often be placed centrally within the train for the guard.

Merthyr and Brecon. Inwards local services from these points arrived at the south face of the island platform, in company with main-line services to London, Bristol, Gloucester and Hereford. The north face was used for Eastern Valley departures and main-line starting services.

The bay platform at the east end of the down platform, which had direct access out to the station approach, catered for horse-boxes, livestock, and perishable traffic such as fruit and vegetables, flowers and fish, though it could be used for a local passenger train in an emergency.

In January 1896, a new, fast service to Paddington began operation. This was the 'Red Dragon', with which we were familiar when re-introduced in the 1950s. The train started from Swansea at 8.30 a.m. (as in the 1950s) with five corridor coaches, and took on a dining car at Cardiff (again as it did in the 50s). It ran forward from Cardiff hauled by a tank engine to Newport, where it changed engines to a Dean 'Single', two of which were allocated to High Street depot; of these, No.3042 *Frederick Saunders* worked the first train. The engine returned from Paddington with the 3.35 p.m. service, known as 'The Flying Welshman', working as far as Newport. The other 4–2–2 worked the 9.30 a.m. Newport to Swindon via Gloucester and, due to the onerous nature of working to London and back via Bath, the train crews worked these two services on alternate days.

Locomotive changing at Newport on main-line services ceased with the opening of the Badminton cut-off in 1903. With the new route, the distance travelled by train engines on London services was reduced, whilst the engines themselves had become more powerful, enabling them to work through to Cardiff. The allocation of Dean 'Singles' to Newport came to an end.

In 1906, the *GWR Magazine* carried a detailed account of operations at Newport station, stating that at that time there were around 50 main-line passenger services in each direction, with a few starting and terminating at Newport. Of trains proceeding west to Cardiff, about a dozen ran through to Swansea and West Wales. There were six or seven London expresses, and through trains or carriages to and from Manchester, Liverpool, Birkenhead, Newcastle, Birmingham and Portsmouth. Additionally, several North & West services passed over the Maindee Junctions, running between Pontypool Road and Bristol, avoiding Newport station.

Another 30 local passenger services per day ran to the Western Valleys (Ebbw Vale, Brynmawr), the Sirhowy Valleys (Tredegar, Nantybwch), and the Brecon & Merthyr lines (Rhymney, Brecon, Pontypridd, Caerphilly and Merthyr), including some steam 'motor

Old Oak 'Castle' No.5087 *Tintern Abbey* moving slowly past East box on the new Down Main with the 7.55 a.m. Paddington to Swansea on Saturday, 22nd April 1961, during the first days of the revised signalling layout work. The signalman was monitoring the passage of the train from the box window, with loudhailers in position to broadcast a message to passing engine crews if necessary. This train conveyed a Restaurant Buffet and a Restaurant car near the front to provide the passengers with breakfast, morning coffee, and perhaps an early lunch. The engine worked to Swansea with this train though the Old Oak crew left the engine at Cardiff – and was scheduled to return to Paddington from Swansea with the 6.50 p.m. Neyland, running via Gloucester. *Tintern Abbey*, No.4067, was the last of the 'Star' to 'Castle' converts, emerging from Swindon factory in December 1940, and allocated to Old Oak; the engine stayed there until January 1962, when she was transferred to Llanelly.

car' services. On the Eastern Valleys, some 15 trains per day ran to Pontypool Crane Street and Blaenavon, a number going on to Brynmawr.

In all, some 200 passenger train movements were carried out at the station daily in 1906, including empty stock movements, while about 150 goods services ran through each day. This level of activity, exacerbated by the movement of local trains across the station between arrival and departing points, and movements to and from the engine shed, caused considerable delays to the running of through trains, passenger and goods. It was therefore decided at the end of the 1900s to construct a new Hillfield Tunnel (qv) alongside the existing one. Completed by 1912, this considerably eased train working through Newport and enabled the Valley trains to be better segregated from the main line, though departing Valley trains from the down bay still posed a problem in crossing, either at the east or west end of the tunnels, to the Western Valley line. At this time, Newport Tunnel box was renamed Newport West.

'Austerity' 2–8–0 No.90201 from Canton shed with a down class 'H' freight, nearing High Street station on Saturday, 10th May 1958, probably with a working from Severn Tunnel Jct. By this year, the Welsh sheds housed the majority of these engines on the Western Region, with the greatest concentration at Canton (around 14), four at Ebbw Jct., and similar numbers at Pontypool Road and Carmarthen.

'15XX' 0–6–0T No.1506 (Pill shed) working a down transfer freight from East Usk Jct. yard to Alexandra Dock Jct. at Newport East on Wednesday, 20th March 1957. East Usk yard was situated at the junction with the Uskmouth branch – where there were several important industrial sites in addition to Uskmouth power station – about a mile to the east of High Street on the south side of the main lines. Ebbw Jct. shed had one example of this class of ten engines in 1957 – No.1509 – whilst Nos. 1506 and 1507 were stationed within the dock area at Pill shed. It was unusual to see a Pill engine on such work, and it may be that No.1506 was being run in following attention at Ebbw Jct. shops.

On Saturday, 14th September 1957, No.6318 from Pontypool Road shed (formerly from Ebbw Jct.) approaching High Street with a class 'F' down empty mineral wagon train. These vehicles would be heading for the valleys, where coal production was already decreasing; some 32 million tons had been carried by the company from collieries in South Wales in 1938, though by 1953 this figure had fallen to 23 million. Far less coal was being taken to the docks (for export or bunkering) than hitherto, though a greater percentage of that being conveyed by rail was being taken into England (some 6 million tons in 1953), increasing the need for mainline marshalling facilities.

Towards the end of the 1920s, considerable work took place at Newport on most aspects of the operation. The loading dock on the north side of the station was made into a platform (No.8) and used for Valley trains, with a scissors crossover at its west end connecting to the line serving the north face of the island platform (Nos.6/7), with another scissors between the two lines outside the West box. The island platform itself was considerably increased in length at the west end, and the scissors crossover connecting with the up through road moved westwards to bisect the new length.

Signalling was modernised, the existing boxes having been in operation since the 1880 redevelopment. The Middle box was now closed, and its operations transferred to the West box, which received a new frame in 1927, and the boxes were rebuilt at both West and East in 1928. The new boxes contained the new Ferreira-Insell electrically-operated mechanisms, East with 84 levers and West with 125. In this system, a 4-position lever combined those operations necessary to set and signal a required movement, in conjunction with track circuiting. The first movement released the lock (if track circuit clear), the second set the points and released another lock, and the third set the signal; a similar sequence operated in reverse to reset the signal and track. Reversible working was provided for Valley trains to both arrive and depart from the north face of the island platform and the new platform 8, and use of the down platform bay (No.3) for departing Valley trains was largely discontinued.

New station facilities were also provided, and the station facade completely transformed. Served from Cambrian Road (Devon Place), the down side had a new five-storey building, completed in 1930. The ground (road and rail level) floor contained the booking hall, enquiry office, refreshment room, waiting room, and toilets, cloakroom, parcels and other platform offices. On the first floor were the dining room, with accommodation for 200 diners, kitchen, smoking and writing rooms, with toilets and cloakroom. The second floor was a self-contained area for use as club premises and, when new, was taken by the County and Monmouth Club.

The third and fourth floors were equipped as offices, housing the Newport Divisional Superintendent (Traffic) and Newport District Goods Manager and their staffs. Newport was also the headquarters for the Newport Locomotive Division, whose sheds ranged from Severn Tunnel Jct. in the east to Tondu in the west, and from Pontrilas and Pontypool Road to Aberdare in the north. It was also the headquarters for the Newport Engineering Division, which stretched from Chepstow to Pyle and from Pontypool Road to Hirwaun, together with many inclusive lines and branches.

By the late 1930s, some 550 passenger and goods movements took place through High Street station daily. In the summer of 1939, nine Paddington expresses called at the station on weekdays with a further three on Saturdays, with four down and three up services on Sundays. Cross-country trains continued to serve a wide variety of destinations, with daily services to and from Manchester and Liverpool (LMS), Newcastle and Hull (LNE), Portsmouth and Brighton (SR), together with GWR services to Birmingham, Birkenhead and Torbay. On summer Saturdays there were additional trains to Bournemouth, Weymouth, Newquay and other holiday locations. The established stopping services continued to serve the Bristol, Gloucester and Hereford lines, while local services served Monmouth, Brecon, the Eastern and Western and Sirhowy Valleys, though some other Valley services had by now been withdrawn.

Wartime saw a reduction of the regular passenger timetable but military traffic more than filled in the gaps created. Passenger traffic rapidly picked up after the war and there was a sustained gradual increase in patronage during the 1950s before the motor-car gained dominance. By the late 1950s, London trains were more frequent than in 1938, with 12 down and 11 up weekday services, and 7 down and 10 up on Sundays. Cross-country trains continued at much the same level on weekdays, but summer Saturday traffic continued its expansion with through trains to Blackpool, Filey Holiday Camp, and Cornwall. A new Pullman service from and to Paddington began in 1955, leaving London at 9.55 a.m. and Swansea at 4.35pm.

Landore 'Castle' No.5062 *Earl of Shaftesbury* on the down 'South Wales Pullman' (Train F14), 8.50 a.m. Paddington to Swansea', approaching Newport station on Tuesday, 9th May 1961. The train comprised an eight-coach set of Pullman vehicles, incorporating First and Second class Parlour and Kitchen cars and a Brake Second at each end. The engine was four months out of Swindon after a 'Heavy Intermediate' repair. When Landore was closed for dieselisation in June 1961, its 'Castles' were split between Neath and Llanelly, both depots having a working to London. The Llanelly engines covered most of the work west of Swansea.

Newton Abbot '28XX' 2–8–0 No.2881 approaching platform No.1 at High Street with the 8.55 a.m. Taunton to Cardiff express on Saturday, 17th September 1955, the penultimate day of the summer timetable. Although fitted with the 4ft 7½in wheels of freight and shunting locomotives, the '28s' were quite capable of sustained speeds up to about 45 mph, and although a good engine could travel faster, the resulting hammer-blow could be detrimental to trackwork.

In the last days of the old signalling layout at Newport, Landore 'Castle' No.4090 *Dorchester Castle* is seen approaching platform No.6 (just renumbered from 1/2) at High Street with Train F15, the 8.55 am. Paddington to Pembroke Dock, on 18th April 1961. Signals were kept at danger, and trains hand-signalled through the layout from the ground, though two loudhailers were available to the signalman to pass instructions to crews or flagmen. No.4090 was the second 'Castle' to be fitted with a double chimney, in April 1957, a year after No.7018. As a double-chimney engine, she went to Old Oak, where her distinguished performance surpassed even that of No.7018, then moved on to Landore in August 1959, and to Carmarthen in the following month. After a 'Heavy Intermediate' repair at Swindon, No.4090 was transferred to Landore in November 1960 for top link working to Paddington. Her final move was to Neath, before dieselisation of the South Wales main line deprived us of the sight and sound of Landore 'Castles' in all their glory.

However, in 1961, this was replaced by the new Blue Pullman diesel service, which, because of the poor loading on the original train, was reversed in operation to start from the Swansea end at 6.30 a.m., returning from London at 4.55 p.m. The success of the up service was overwhelming and seats had to be reserved in advance to have any hope of getting on.

The requirement to move huge volumes of iron ore from Newport Docks to the new Llanwern Steelworks, as well as coal from the Valleys pits, caused the redevelopment of the tracks between Alexandra Dock Jct., High Street and Llanwern in 1961, followed by the introduction of Multiple Aspect Signalling in 1962. Because of the importance and widespread effect of this development, it is covered in a separate section.

The effect of these modifications on Newport station itself began in April 1961, when the new track layout began implementation. The up and down main lines were now to run either side of the island platform, and the former down platform would become isolated. Platforms were renumbered from the north side, the original No.8 becoming No.1, Nos. 6/7 became 2/3, Nos. 4/5 remained the same, and Nos. 1/2 became No.6. Though some trains were routed in the new way initially on an experimental basis, because of the presence of local services on the north face of the island platform,

Six 'Kings' came to Canton for the winter 1960 services, and took over the top turns to Paddington and Shrewsbury, though ex-works 'Castles' and 'Britannias' were still being utilised for such duties. No.6019 *King Henry V* of Canton shed is seen here entering No.6 platform with the down 'Capitals United', the 3.55 p.m. Paddington to Swansea, in May 1961, with stock in chocolate and cream livery. The scheduled up duty earlier that day for the 'King' was the 10.0 a.m. from Cardiff, the 'Red Dragon'. At the time of her transfer to Canton, No.6019 was receiving a 'Heavy General' at Swindon works, and so was in excellent condition when she arrived at her new home. Although being hauled by the more powerful 'Kings', the South Wales expresses were not retimed, and so it was only when the trains were running late, or were overloaded, that the engines were able to show their true worth. Unlike 'Castles' and 'Britannias', the 'Kings' were not permitted west of Canton, and an engine change was therefore required at Cardiff for services beyond; their utilisation was therefore low.

Aberdare '28XX' No.2831 bringing a class 'F' train of empty mineral wagons along the down through road at High Street station on Saturday, 25th May 1957. This working may have been from Salisbury, on which service a number of the early '28XX' engines were rostered in October 1906, and continued into the 1960s. No.2831 was transferred into the area in 1931, and spent time at Severn Tunnel, Aberdare and Ebbw Jct. sheds before moving back to Aberdare in 1944, remaining there until she was withdrawn in 1960. In addition to the Salisbury turns, Aberdare regularly used its '28s' to Moreton Cutting (Didcot) at this time.

No.70028 *Royal Star* taking the up 'Red Dragon' (7.30 a.m. Carmarthen) out of No.5 platform, High Street, and onto the Up Main on Saturday, 2nd May 1959. The train number '066' was a short-lived winter 1958/9 identification for the morning Carmarthen service; it had been '720' throughout the 'fifties until summer 1958, when '726' was used. Subsequently it was numbered '031' in summer 1959, and was 'A35' from summer 1960. This was the Canton 'top' turn of the day, and the engine was always resplendent. It was also one of the two longest turns on the Western Region – some 340 miles – between coaling; leaving Cardiff General at 10.0 a.m., the engine spent a couple of hours at Ranelagh Bridge before returning with the 3.55 p.m. Paddington to Swansea, where coal would be taken. It was sometimes touch-and-go whether the engine would have sufficient to reach Landore, so, immediately before leaving Canton shed for the station, the engine (and that of the 8.0 a.m. Cardiff on a similar diagram) would be taken back to the coaling stage to be topped up, replacing the coal used in preparation.

Right: Another view of the 'Red Dragon' behind No 70028 on the same day as it accelerated away from High Street and onto the Usk viaduct.

the new working arrangements had to be delayed in implementation.

With far greater management interest in promoting the revenue to be generated by the huge tonnages of freight traffic into and out of Llanwern, it was announced that the local passenger services would be withdrawn and, against huge public opposition, both remaining Valleys services were withdrawn in April 1962, with the Brecon service following in December, the Sirhowy service having been cut back to Risca in 1959. Much play was made by the protesters of the developing town of Cwmbran, and this requirement was met in later years by re-opening the station there and serving with main-line trains between Pontypool Road and Newport.

December 1962 was a huge milestone in the signalling history of Newport, when full multiple-aspect signalling was implemented throughout the area, and the activities of the two station signal boxes, East and West, joined all the others in the area in being transferred into the new Newport Panel box, located at the east end of the down platform.

Though the new layout had the desired effect of properly segregating passenger and freight traffic through the Newport area, and generally reducing confliction, it was not achieved without a further

'9F' 2–10–0 No.92220 *Evening Star* departing from platform No.4 with the up 'Red Dragon' on 27th June 1960, carrying the 'A35' number. The engine earmarked for the 10.30 a.m. Cardiff to Portsmouth was on standby each day to cover a failure of the locomotive rostered for the 10.0 a.m. departure (the 'Red Dragon'), and, whether by accident or design, No.92220 eventually found itself on the 10.0 a.m. earlier in June 1960. The run was non-stop from Newport to Paddington, and the Class '9' was so much in control that an effort to avoid a very early arrival at Paddington had to be made, to enable the luncheon servings to be completed. On this diagram, the engine returned with the down 'Capitals', the 3.55 p.m. Paddington.

Bath Road 'Castle' No.5057 *Earl Waldegrave* running through the down middle road at Newport High Street on Thursday, 20th June 1957, with the 3.45 p.m. Paddington to Fishguard Harbour. Very few service passenger trains ran through Newport or Cardiff without calling, and those that did were invariably Fishguard boat trains. The 3.45 p.m. Paddington service was shown in the service and public timetables as 'calls to take up only' from both stations, and would probably only have called at Newport had the station supervisor there advised Control that passengers for Ireland were waiting. Otherwise, it called only at Swansea and Clarbeston Road en route for passengers. The 3.55 p.m. Paddington was ten minutes behind this service at Newport, and also carried through coaches for Fishguard, though unlike the 3.45 p.m. it called at all main stations en route. The 3.45 p.m. did, nevertheless, call at Cardiff to change enginemen. This service connected with the 11.45 p.m. steamer from Fishguard to Cork. The engine was about halfway between heavy repair cycles, and thus found itself wandering away from its 'prime' routes, though after the next 'Heavy General' it would doubtless be back on the top link Bristol & London work.

Ex-works Canton 'Hall', No.5934 *Linden Hall*, departing from No.4/5 platform with the 10.30 a.m. Cardiff to Portsmouth & Southsea train No.058, on Tuesday, 18th April 1961, with a six-coach formation and tail traffic. The first two coaches were Collett large-window types. This turn was diagrammed for one of Canton's two 'Manors' at this time, but was usually worked by a good 'Hall', or a 'Britannia'. The engine ran through to Salisbury with this train, and returned thence with the 4.17 p.m. (the 2.45 p.m. Portsmouth & Southsea to Bristol), and the 10.50 p.m. Bristol to Cardiff vacuum freight in time to work the same duty the following day.

Radyr had four '72XX' 2–8–2Ts for working coal (including loco coal) services to Severn Tunnel Jct. or Salisbury. On 18th May 1961, No.7252 was bringing a a loaded class 'H' coal train along the up through road at High Street station. South Wales' collieries supplied loco coal to most GWR/WR depots, and also to Southern Railway/Region depots in the south and west of England. When steam traction diminished as the primary form of motive power on BR lines, the NCB were able to crush the large coal and supply it in treated form to the new Spencer steelworks, Llanwern, as prime coking coal.

The London end of platform No.2 (later No.6) provided an excellent vantage point for photographing up services departing from Newport. Here Canton 'Britannia' No.70020 *Mercury* was leaving High Street with the 8.0 a.m. Neyland (12 noon Cardiff) to Paddington on Wednesday, 20th March 1957. This train carried vehicles from many points during the winter 1956/7 period, with a standard formation of five from Swansea (including two dining vehicles), three from Neyland, one from Fishguard Harbour, and three from Pembroke Dock; this diversity reflected the formations of Welsh expresses of the 1920s and 30s, which was no longer to be found to quite the same degree on West Country or Northern services out of Paddington by this time. The 'Britannia' had taken over at Cardiff, and would return there with the 5.55 p.m. Paddington to Carmarthen service, the down 'Red Dragon'. As from January 1957, Canton received the full WR allocation of 15 'Britannias' in recognition of the better level of use and acceptance they had received at Cardiff than at other WR depots.

Landore 'Castle' No.7021 *Haverfordwest Castle* leaving Newport platform No.4/5 with train No.790, the 8.10 a.m. Swansea to York, via Banbury, on Saturday, 14th September 1957; on the previous day, this stock had formed the 12.20 p.m. York to Swansea and, as can be seen, was formed very largely of ex-LNER vehicles. The Western Region supplied a train that worked to Newcastle on Fridays, returning from there (at 10.8 a.m.) on Saturdays. These were the descendants of the 'Ports-to-Ports' services introduced in May 1906, which connected ports in the North-East of England with those in South Wales (running via Barry and the Vale of Glamorgan line), especially for the convenience of seamen. Originally, these took the Banbury & Cheltenham route to and from Gloucester, and in the 1920s and 30s were worked by Banbury '43XXs', and 'Manors' for the last few months of peace. The trains were withdrawn upon the outbreak of war in 1939, although one would have thought there would have been a great need for such a service during the hostilities. When re-introduced in 1946, they were routed via Didcot West and the Severn Tunnel. The Landore engine was still rostered through to Banbury (due at 12.52 p.m.), as it had been in 1946, and returned with the 10.8 a.m. Newcastle or 12.20 p.m. York (4.34 p.m. Banbury) to Swansea, due 9.25 p.m. Until 1955, this train ran every weekday, but from that year ran Mondays, Fridays and Saturdays only, and Fridays and Saturdays only from 1957. There were also services to and from York and Newcastle via Gloucester and the LMR.

'9F' 2–10–0s were first allocated to the Western Region in February/March 1954, when Nos.92000–07 went new to Ebbw Jct., and after modification began work on Newport Docks to Ebbw Vale iron ore trains. From the latter part of 1958, new double-chimney examples arrived on the Region, and were to be found at Old Oak, Banbury, St Philip's Marsh, Laira and Canton, later moving to Ebbw Jct. Regular Standard Class '9' operation on passenger duties in South Wales on summer Saturdays commenced in 1959, and they were commonly found on cross-country passenger duties; their power and acceleration was a great boon to recovering time, whilst on heavier gradients such as Filton bank and the Severn Tunnel, their performance was very impressive. No.92207 came out of Swindon works in June 1959, and was allocated to St. Philip's Marsh; she is seen here arriving at and leaving the new No. 4/5 platform with the Saturdays-only 9.20 a.m. Swansea to Brockenhurst service (train No.265) on 27th June 1959. This was the second Saturday of the train's operation, which continued until 5th September.

The 8.0 a.m. Neyland to Paddington (train A58) leaving Newport behind Canton 'King' No.6004 *King George III* on 24th September 1960, in their first month of operation. 'Kings' Nos.6003, 6004, 6018, 6019, 6023 and 6028 were allocated for the winter 1960/1 service, beginning on 13th September, and were joined a year later by Nos.6010 and 6024, when the Canton 'Britannias' were moved to the LMR. The arrangement was cut short by main-line dieselisation, and the first (No.6003) was transferred to Old Oak in January 1962, followed by 6019 in March, with the remainder either condemned or transferred to Old Oak in June and July of that year.

Returning home after repair at Caerphilly, Severn Tunnel Jct's '51XX' 2–6–2T No.5155 is seen running through the up middle road at High Street station with a mineral train on Saturday, 14th September 1957. The engine was transferred from Stourbridge Jct. to Severn Tunnel Jct. in 1953, and was withdrawn in January 1960 after thirty years of service.

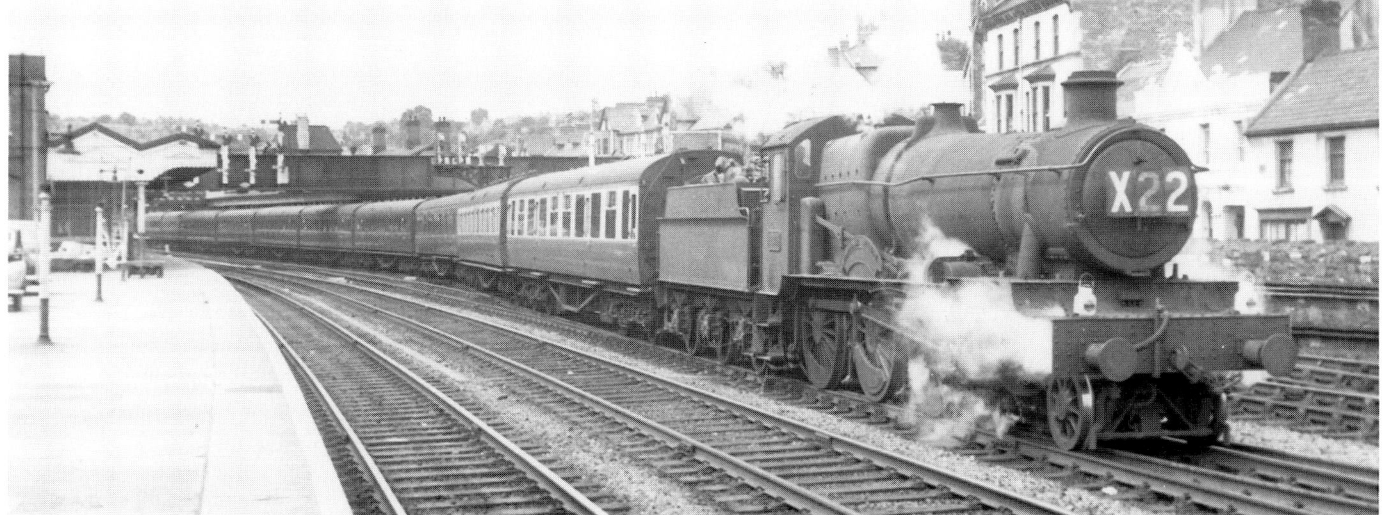

'Manor' No.7805 *Broome Manor* departing from No.5 platform with an up excursion (X22) to Bristol on Saturday, 27th June 1959. No.7805 was the first allocation of the class to Canton, arriving first in May 1958 but was quickly transferred (with others) to Laira for pilot work over the South Devon banks during the summer timetable. No.7820 also arrived ex-works from Swindon, but was again hastily moved to Laira. Both engines were returned to Canton in September 1958 along with 7809, though the latter was soon transferred to Gloucester. Nos.7805 and 7820 remained there, and at Cardiff East Dock, until the spring of 1963. The official allocations for 'Manors' between June and December 1958 contain some unaccountable inaccuracies, and do not fully show the shed movements of the class.

A portrait of Pontypool Road 'Grange' No.6840 *Hazeley Grange*, seen on its way through High Street station with an up 'H' class freight on Saturday, 20th June 1957. She was passing under the footbridge that previously crossed the station, running from the station approach across to Mill Street, from where Western Welsh and Red & White bus services departed for the Western and Sirhowy Valleys. When introduced in the latter 1930s, the '68s' were scheduled almost entirely for freight work, though they were a common sight on summer Saturday express passenger duties. In the 1950s, their daily work was around 80% freight throughout the system, although certain areas – the West Country, for example – used more of their allocation on passenger-rated duties. The tall, 1930s station building on the left dominates the scene.

casualty, that of the excellent down main platform with all its facilities. With the withdrawal of the local services, main-line trains began to use the two faces of the island platform; all passengers joining and alighting at Newport had to cross the footbridge from the entrance on the down platform, a situation which still exists.

Management of railway activities underwent a substantial change between 1963–5 when the Newport District Traffic Superintendent's Office was amalgamated with that of the Swansea and Cardiff Superintendents under the Divisional Manager, Cardiff. Newport control was also closed, and became part of the Divisional control at Cardiff. In the development of local ground management, station masters disappeared in the mid-1960s, and were replaced by Area Managers. Because of the size and level of activity of the Newport area, two Area Managers were needed, one at High Street, controlling the area east of the tunnels, including Newport Goods, and the other the area west of the tunnels, including Ebbw Jct. and Pill engine sheds and all BR activities on the docks.

A new ticket office and travel centre opened in the former booking hall in 1973, but, other than this, the station seems to have changed little since the mid-sixties. Lack of space in the right place seems to preclude the installation of escalators which are much required to facilitate transfer of passengers between platforms.

Prior to the strengthening of the Rumney River bridge on the eastern outskirts of Cardiff, 'King' workings into South Wales were rare. The engines were cleared to run via the Severn Tunnel as far as Cardiff (including Canton shed) from 1952, though with speed restrictions imposed; 'Castles' and 'Britannias' were, however, permitted to run at higher speeds. On Saturday, 10th May 1958, Laira's No.6008 *King James II* was working a Bath Road turn involving the 9.5 a.m. Bristol to Cardiff; returning as diagrammed with the 12.32 p.m. Cardiff (11.5 a.m. Swansea) to Penzance train as far as Plymouth; this was done to work the 'unbalanced King' home.

'Saints' were a familiar sight on express passenger services at Newport from 1907, and increasingly on secondary services with the expansion of the 'Castles' in the early 1930s. At Newport, Ebbw Jct. maintained a trio of them from 1932 into the Second World War, and in the final days of the class had Nos.2936 and 2979 allocated until their withdrawal in 1951. No.2927 *Saint Patrick* from Swindon shed is seen here at platform No.4/5 with a Cardiff to Bristol stopping service in early 1951. She was withdrawn from traffic in December of that year.

No.3703 leaving platform No.8 with the 4.8 p.m. on 14th September 1957. With the 1961 remodelling, this platform became No.1, and was the only 'single'-length through platform at High Street; the remainder were 'double'-length.

Pontypool Road's No.3703 standing at No.8 platform with a train for the Eastern Valleys, the 4.8 p.m. to Blaenavon (Low Level) on 14th September 1957. Two years later, this service was scheduled for DMU operation.

Aberdare's '42XX' 2–8–0T No.5237 making its way through No.8 platform at Newport with the 2.50 p.m. Aberdare to Severn Tunnel Jct. coal train on Tuesday, 14th April 1959. Aberdare services had two routes they could take off the Vale of Neath line: via Sirhowy Jct. and the Sirhowy Valley line, or via Penar Jct. and the Western Valley line, both of which converged at Risca to enable a call at Rogerstone yard if necessary. After the 0–6–0PTs, the '42s' were the most common tank in the Newport Locomotive District in 1959, with 94 examples; of these, 24 were at Ebbw. Jct and 18 at Pill, whilst the others were spread between Severn Tunnel Jct., Pontypool Road, Aberbeeg, Aberdare, Canton, Llantrisant and Tondu.

Transitional signalling at Newport, showing gantries at the east end of the island platform (Nos.2 and 4) on 15th April 1961. Bi-directional running was in force along both sides of the island platform.

Diesel railcar No.4 standing at No.8 platform on 9th April 1955. Built in 1934, No.4 was one of the 44-seat buffet cars introduced for the Birmingham & Cardiff services via Gloucester. In January 1947 it was transferred from Stourbridge to Newport, then on to Landore in the following May. It returned to Newport nearly four years later, and was utilised on return trips to Bridgend in the morning and Swansea in the afternoon. Later, it worked on the severn Tunnel Jct., Chepstow & Monmouth turn on which it is probably seen here. The car was withdrawn in July 1958.

'2251' 0-6-0 No.2275 standing at No.6 platform with the 2.0 p.m. Brecon to Newport service, consisting of two corridor coaches. No.2275 was allocated to '89A', which covered Oswestry, Moat Lane and Llanidloes sheds, the engine having moved north from Taunton during 1956. No.2275 ran with 3,000-gallon tender No.1522 (Lot A52 of 1902) from 1955 until May 1959, and it is probably that tender seen in this view. Whitaker's automatic token exchange apparatus was fitted on the left-hand side front edge of tenders working over the Barnstaple and Minehead branches, in the position of the dark patch seen here. Although coach-working documents of the 1950s show the train to have been formed of the standard Brake Composite and Van Second of the Brecon & Newport trains, this was strengthened when necessary by the addition of a Second class coach.

During 1962, several of the West & North services ran via Newport High Street, where the engine either ran round (if diesel) or changed (steam). 'Britannia' class 4-6-2 No.70011 *Hotspur* is seen here waiting at No.2/3 platform with a train to Crewe and the north in 1962. By this time, the modernisation scheme had brought each side of the island platform (originally platforms 4/5 and 6/7) into use as the main platforms, with the original up main platform (4/5) now the down main, and the down relief (originally 6/7, renumbered 2/3) now the up main, with No.8 (now renumbered 1) for local services.

The evening sun highlighting No.5036 *Lyonshall Castle* alongside platform No.6 with the 2.55 p.m. Paddington to Swansea on Tuesday, 9th May 1961. An Old Oak engine, No.5036 was fitted with a double chimney as late as December 1960, and was withdrawn less than two years later, in September 1962. Platform No.6, formerly Nos. 1 and 2, had been renumbered under the first stage of the multiple aspect signalling scheme three weeks earlier. The 'Bay' platform, originally No.3, can be seen on the far side of the canopy, with part of the goods station title board visible beyond.

Pontypool Road WD 'Austerity' (8F) 2–8–0 No.90192 on 20th March 1957 rumbling along the up main one afternoon with an up 'H' class mineral, probably destined for the Severn Tunnel or Gloucester route. All the vehicles appear to have been of wooden designs.

Canton 'King' No.6019 *King Henry V* pausing at platform No.6 with the down 'Capitals United Express' (Train 'F55'), the 3.55 p.m. Paddington to Fishguard Harbour. Despite the name to indicate a link between the English and Welsh capitals, the service conveyed coaches for both Neyland and Fishguard Harbour, with the main part of the train running to Swansea. The 'Capitals United' name had been introduced in 1956, and a front summary page of the public timetables from that time prominently announced 'Refreshment Car Service – London and Cardiff', giving the arrival and departure times of both up and down trains, but with no mention of the calls at Badminton and Newport en route, or of the stations served to the west, although the main pages did indicate the full arrangements.

In complete contrast to its normal duties, Ebbw Jct '94XX' No.8499 is seen here departing from platform No.1/2 with the down 'South Wales Pullman' in the summer of 1959. The train engine, a Landore 'Castle', failed at Llanwern, and the 0–6–0 tank hauled the 8.50 a.m. Paddington with its eight Pullman cars as far as Cardiff General, where a 4–6–0 took over for the remainder of the journey to Swansea. The train was due to leave Newport at 12.25 p.m., so the train standing in the up platform was probably the 8.0 a.m. Neyland.

No.6004 *King George III* arriving at platform No.4/5 at High Street with the 8.0 a.m. Neyland to Paddington on 24th September 1960, during the first month of 'King' working from Canton to Paddington. Dieselisation on the West Country route had ousted the last of the 'Kings' from Laira in that month, though Canton's six all came from Old Oak. With electrification work on the ex-LMS route to Birmingham in hand, an hourly service (plus additional peak trains) worked over the ex-Great Western route from Paddington, demanded the rest of the engines, shared between Old Oak and Stafford Road sheds.

A 'classic' mixed goods train, with '43XX' 2–6–0 No.6341 (from Gloucester shed) running along the down middle road at High Street with a partially vacuum-fitted class 'D' express freight on Saturday, 24th September 1960. At this time, there were still about 120 of this class in traffic, though all had gone by the end of 1964. The combination of a six-coupled engine with general merchandise opens and covered goods, together with coal or empties, had been a familiar sight for at least 80 years by this time, though its days were numbered.

Western Valleys services latterly ran from platform No.7, at the west end of the island platform's northern face. Aberbeeg's '94XX' 0–6–0PT No.8494 is seen here with the five-coach 11.5 a.m. Newport to Brynmawr on Saturday, 14th September 1957. Peak-time Valley services were mostly formed of five coaches, although off-peak trains at this time often comprised three vehicles. Here the leading vehicles are a 'B Set' with recessed guard's doors (9ft 3in stock).

HIGH STREET ENGINE SHED

The engine shed at Newport High Street opened in August 1854, some four years after the opening of the line. The engine shed was part of a larger complex which included a fitting shop and carriage and wagon shops, located in sidings developed to the north-west of the station, in the area later to become known as Godfrey Road Sidings. Lyons and Mountford, in their *Great Western Engine Sheds 1837–1947*, show a 4-road shed, 198ft long by 65ft 9in wide, constructed of stone with a gable-end, slated roof. A 45ft turntable was provided together with the usual facilities for offices and stores, cleaning and sand. The broad-gauge tracks were converted to standard in 1872 and, probably partly on account of the effect of this, the depot underwent improvements to facilities and layout in 1879. The original coaling plant was removed and a new coal stage with water tank over was installed, sited closer to the shed on the northern edge of the yard. The turntable was resited on the road serving the stores, just before the shed entrance.

As at January 1901, a total of 114 engines were shown allocated to Newport, but only the main-line element of this allocation was based at High Street. Those engines concerned with dock and yard shunting and tripping were based at Bolt Street, a large depot and works situated near Dock Street. Bolt Street's allocation would have been made up of many of the eighty-seven 0–6–0ST types allocated to Newport, leaving High Street with 4–6–0 No.36, '3521' Class 4–4–0s Nos.3532, 3533 and 3552, Dean 'Single' 4–4–0s 3042 and 3071, plus a variety of 0–6–0 types and passenger tanks. One of the 0–6–0s would pilot the Dean 'Single' (probably to Patchway) when the up 'Red Dragon' was over the load for a single engine. Brecon & Merthyr Railway engines working into Newport at this time were based at Bassaleg or Brecon.

With the development of the Monmouthshire coalfield, a larger allocation of mineral engines was needed in the Newport area, which could not be met from existing depots. In 1915, a new depot was therefore opened by the GWR at Ebbw Jct. (qv), and the High Street depot was closed and demolished the following year. The area where once the engine shed had stood became part of the carriage sidings, where vehicles off incoming services were held until their next working, plus spare vehicles for strengthening, and spare sets of coaches. This arrangement survived until the end of steam, the area being known as Godfrey Road Sidings.

Following the closure of Ebbw Jct. depot in October 1963, Godfrey Road again became a stabling point for engines working in the Newport area, and this role has been continued to the present day; a contingent of the new EWS 66XXX diesels can always be seen standing in the present depot where once broad-gauge engines stood. The original carriage and wagon stone building remains on the north side of the yard, while at the east end of the station, the original stone boundary wall with Mill Street is still in place, possibly having been repointed in a few places over its 150 years.

'2251' 0–6–0 No.3219 at work in the Godfrey Road carriage sidings at Newport West on 14th September 1957, with the buildings in the Civic Centre forming the backdrop. This section of the sidings originally housed the carriage & wagon repair works and facilities.

At the west end of the station stood Newport West box, at the rear of which was the west end of Godfrey Road sidings. This was the site of the original four-road Newport High Street main-line engine shed, the turntable for which was retained, and can be seen on the right; the shed closed with the opening of Ebbw Jct. in July 1915. This view shows Class '2' 2–6–0 No.46520 passing West box with the 2.0 p.m. Brecon to Newport service on Saturday, 17th April 1954, with an additional Second in front of the usual pair of coaches. Between November 1952 and May 1953, twenty-two light 2–6–0s of this Swindon-built Ivatt design (Nos.46503–24) were allocated new to Oswestry for use on the Central Wales section.

Unusually, 'Britannia' No.70023 *Venus* was carrying the 'Capitals United' board for the 3.55 p.m. Paddington to Fishguard Harbour above its front buffer beam, with train number '724' in the normal position, on Saturday, 30th May 1959.

The 'Capitals United', 3.55 p.m. Paddington to Swansea and the west, with No.92220 in charge. As recalled in the Cardiff volume, No.92220 frequently found its way onto the up 'Red Dragon' in June 1960, despite its unsuitability for high-speed running. It performed very well, and all the link enginemen wanted their turn on it. Indeed, No.92220 continued with the 10.0 a.m. Cardiff and 3.55 p.m. Paddington duty until the locomotive management learnt of its use, and forbade further rostering, fearing damage at high speeds. This, however, was not implemented until the head of Canton Loco LDC had had his turn, and on 1st July 1960, Eddie Broom was on the footplate of *Evening Star* on its return working to Cardiff; where the crew would be changed, though 92220 continued through to Swansea.

The Great Western built No.3150 in 1906 with a larger (standard No.4) boiler than carried by the preceding '3100' class 2–6–2Ts, and it became the first of a new series. Nos.3151–90 were constructed to a similar design in 1907–08, though with slightly larger cylinders. In 1938, it was decided to rebuild the '3150' class with new boilers and smaller (5ft 3in) wheels, again for banking duties, renumbered as '3100' class. However, the war intervened, and only five engines were completed. Ebbw Jct '3100' No.3103, is seen here shunting stock into the down bay (No.3) platform on 20th June 1957. After October of that year, it was the only survivor of the class, being withdrawn itself in January 1960. A 'Siphon G' and newspaper van are formed behind the engine.

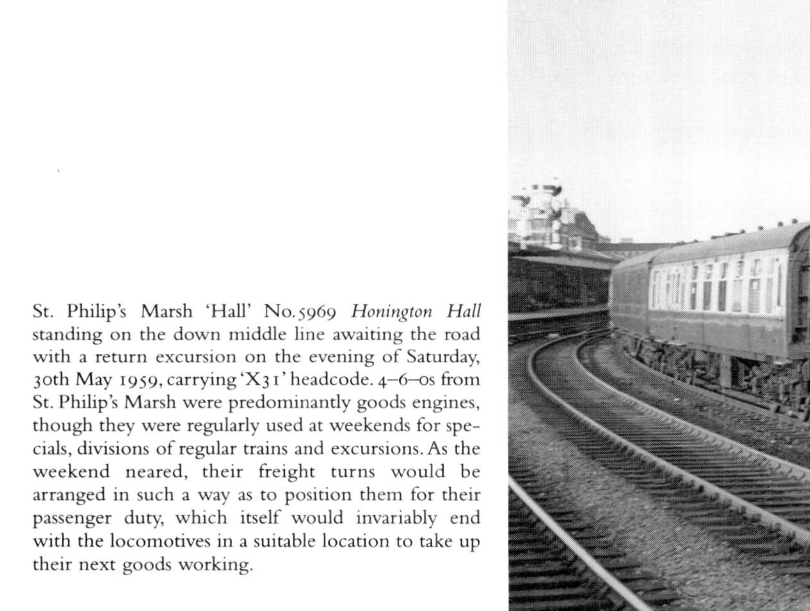

St. Philip's Marsh 'Hall' No.5969 *Honington Hall* standing on the down middle line awaiting the road with a return excursion on the evening of Saturday, 30th May 1959, carrying 'X31' headcode. 4–6–0s from St. Philip's Marsh were predominantly goods engines, though they were regularly used at weekends for specials, divisions of regular trains and excursions. As the weekend neared, their freight turns would be arranged in such a way as to position them for their passenger duty, which itself would invariably end with the locomotives in a suitable location to take up their next goods working.

A view of the main-line portion of the station, looking east on 4th March 1961 with No.6934 *Beachamwell Hall* from Stafford Road shed pausing at High Street with a down express, possibly one of the eleven daily services from Birmingham to Cardiff or West Wales, running via Hereford or Gloucester. No.9488 from Ebbw Jct is seen in the bay with a westbound train, possibly for Cardiff; there were no intermediate stations on that route by this time. High Street goods shed forms a backdrop to this view, with the office block at the far end. The scissors crossover between Up Main and Up Platform lines had been removed in late 1959, and that between the down lines (by the rear of the express) would shortly share the same fate.

A pair of '43s' – No.5335 (Llanelly shed) and 6353 (Canton) – picking up speed on the up middle line at High Street with an up special on Saturday, 14th September 1957. In addition to football and rugby specials, there were many other day excursions for various organisations, and these would often run non-stop through Newport using the middle roads.

Ebbw Jct '2251' No.2227 leaving No.3 bay platform with the 6.55 p.m. Newport to Brecon train on Saturday, 30th May 1959. The journey time for the 47 miles to Brecon was about 2½ hours, and the train ran via Bassaleg, where it joined the Brecon & Merthyr route to Machen, Maesycwmmer, Bargoed, Dowlais Top, Pontsticill Jct. and Talyllyn Jct. Three coaches were obviously required on this occasion.

The same train, 6.55 p.m. Newport, departing this time behind No.46516, from Brecon shed, on 20th June 1957. This was the last train of the day over this route to Brecon. The service again departed from the down bay platform (No.3) with the usual Brake Compo and Van Second formation. Brecon's '465XX' 2–6–0s were diagrammed on the Mid Wales line northwards to Moat Lane and Oswestry, as well as to Newport. The 'Sunshine' stock Van Third behind the engine illustrates a very low waistline division of red and cream when compared with the following vehicle.

A large number of goods trains passed through the middle roads at Newport station, with around 100 movements in each direction daily during the 1950s. Coal from the 150 or so pits in operation in the latter part of the decade still formed the greatest single commodity, though the iron and steel industry, together with the associated raw materials, provided considerable traffic. This picture shows '28XX' 2–8–0 No.3849 from Canton with a down class 'F' empties on the down middle road at the west end of Newport station on 14th April 1959. Steel wagon stock increasingly predominated on the mineral services.

'Austerity' 2–8–0 No.90573 (88A – Canton) approaching Newport West with a down class 'H' freight on Tuesday, 9th May 1961. The train of bogie vehicles for the conveyance of plate, bar or rod metal and similar loads, was probably bound for Guest, Keens, at Cardiff.

Ebbw Jct. '9F' 2–10–0s Nos.92007 and 92229 at the west end of High Street, on 5th May 1960. By this time, the '9Fs' were seen in some profusion around Newport, with 18 at Ebbw Jct, and 11 at Canton, plus those from Banbury and elsewhere on through freight and summer Saturday passenger trains. No.92229 had been given a clear road through No.1/2 platform with a class 'C' train, whilst No.92007, being overtaken on the down middle road, was making its way to Ebbw Jct. shed attached to a pannier tank.

No.92241 lit by the low evening sun and taking the up middle road with a class 'C' freight on 30th May 1959. Allocated to Old Oak, the engine shows little sign of being recently cleaned. This service – possibly the 4.10 p.m. Swansea to Paddington, an Old Oak turn at the time – was piped throughout, with not less than half of the vehicles operating on the automatic vacuum brake. The use of such heavy engines on faster duties was not unusual, as they had a fair turn of speed when required.

'3100' 2–6–2T No.3103 restarting an East Usk branch to Alexandra Dock Jct. transfer freight at Newport West on 20th June 1957; this conveyed the day's traffic from the Uskmouth branch. Two of the five engines of the '3100' class were in South Wales in the 1950s, though the other (No.3100) had been withdrawn from service at Tondu the previous month. All five were allocated to South Wales sheds when new, but three were transferred to the Wolverhampton Division in the mid-war years.

HIGH STREET GOODS

The goods shed and sidings were constructed as part of the original 1850 development, by Messrs. Hughes & Co. The goods facilities were to the west (town side) of the station on the down side, with a large goods shed and cattle pens at the eastern end. The shed had two loop sidings passing through it, a spur from the southerly line running to the west end of the down passenger platform to terminate against the station building. Trailing connections linked the shed directly with the up and down main lines.

As part of the alterations with the gauge change of 1872, access to and from the depot at the east end was made from the middle road through the passenger station. In the goods shed itself, open platforms were added for handling inwards and outwards sundries traffic, some being later covered. Five yard sidings for full load traffic were also added and the cattle pens were moved to the west end of the depot.

In the redevelopment of 1880, the down passenger platform was considerably lengthened, and the connection from the east end of the goods depot to the main line removed; all access to the depot was now controlled by Newport Tunnel box (the forerunner of Newport West) at the south-west end of the yard. A small yard crane was available towards the west end of the yard, but full load traffic requiring heavier lifts was dealt with at Lliswerry Mileage Yard, on the eastern outskirts of the town.

It had become apparent before the Great War that the depot was becoming inadequate for the amount of traffic on offer. The goods shed problems were exacerbated by the fact that handling took place in two sheds, one of which was the old timber and stone building. In 1926, work began on reconstruction of the goods shed. A new building of three floors, cellar, platform and first floor warehouse was constructed entirely of reinforced concrete, each floor connected by an electric goods lift. The goods shed itself was provided with two platforms, each 400ft. long, with two tracks between, accommodating up to 40 wagons. Up to 120 horse-drawn or motor vehicles could be positioned on the cartage front under cover of awnings on the outer faces of the platforms. Counterbalancing, lifting bridges allowed transfer of goods between the two platforms. Office accommodation, located in the north-east corner, completed the facilities in the new structure. Further minor modifications enabled the depot to eventually hold 47 wagons under cover, with sidings space for 102 more in the yard. A total of 97 cartage vehicles finally operated from the depot collecting and delivering goods traffic in the Newport area.

Newport Goods survived in this form until the early 1970s. In 1969, the goods operations became part of National Carriers Ltd. but in 1972, the British Railways Board disengaged from the whole of its goods sundries business, and the depot was closed. The sidings were recovered in 1973 and the area included in a redevelopment plan to provide a station link road and car park.

Newport goods depot, seen in 1961, with a new MAS signal gantry dominating the foreground. The shed occupied the ground floor, with offices at the far end, and warehousing in the cellars. The cartage front is clearly visible in the centre, with a variety of lorries backed up to the deck. In the right foreground, the yard crane is in use, loading a traller for delivery to a customer. Newport was an important small consignment and wagon load depot, with direct wagons to many other centres, e.g. Paddington, Birmingham and Manchester. The office block beyond the bay platform housed the Newport District Office until 1963.

The Newport goods shed pilot was worked by various pannier types, and was still the preserve of '2021' class engines in the early 1950s, with '57s' taking over as the vintage designs were withdrawn By 1960, it was common for '64XX' class tanks to be rostered, as these were in greater supply after their removal from some of their passenger workings in the area with dieselisation. Ebbw Jct's No.6425 is pictured in the goods yard at High Street, along with the inevitable shunting truck. The turn was quiet in the afternoon, but during the early morning and the evening, the engine would be shunting continuously, berthing and clearing wagons for unloading and/or loading. She would finally work the outwards wagons to Alexandra Dock Jct., where the day had started at about 6.0 a.m. with inwards traffic for the goods shed,.

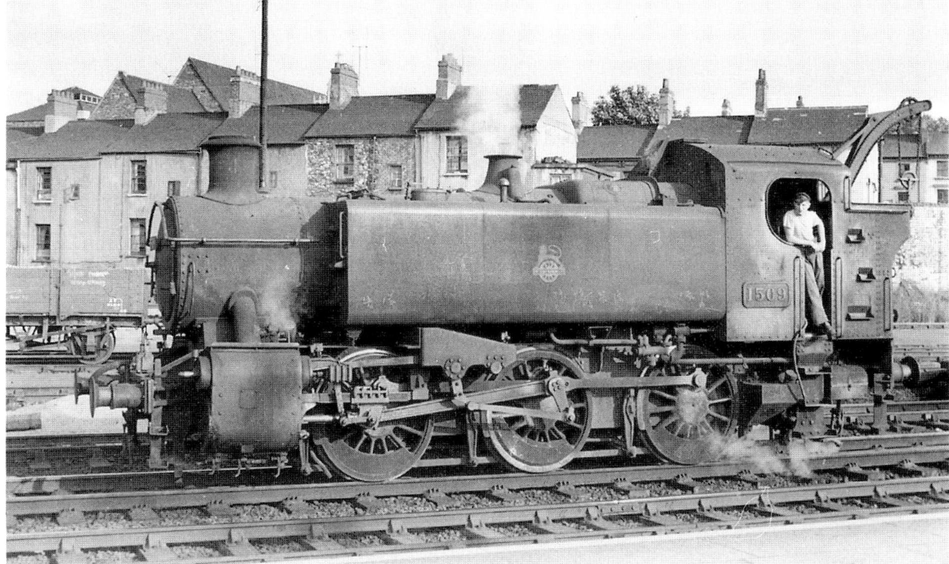

Having completed shunting duties at East Usk, Hawksworth '15XX' 0-6-0PT No.1509, from Ebbw Jct., was waiting for a road through the tunnels on 30th May 1959, on her way back to shed.

Ebbw Jct. '28XX' No.3837 easing along the down middle with empty mineral wagons on 4th March 1961. Ebbw Jct '28XXs' were used on heavy freights from Rogerstone to Oxford (Yarnton) and Newton Abbot (Hackney), and from Alexandra Dock Jct. to Stourbridge Jct., (etc.) together with the balancing down services. The bracket signals on the up platform still controlled the down main and platform lines, although preparation for multiple aspect signalling was under way. The signal 'off' indicates that the freight would cross into the new tunnel, probably bound for Rogerstone.

'56XX' 0-6-2T No.5698 from Aberdare (88J from January 1961 – formerly 86J) making its way through High Street station on 4th March 1961 with a Severn Tunnel Jct. to Aberdare train of empty mineral wagons. Aberdare's '42XXs' and '56XX' worked through to Severn Tunnel Jct. via Rogerstone with loaded coal, returning with eagerly-awaited empties. The shed's '28s' still worked through into England, as they had done for 55 years.

Recently ex-Swindon after a 'Heavy General' repair, Old Oak 'Castle' No.5034 *Corfe Castle* is pictured departing from platform No.1 with train C37, the 7.55 a.m. Penzance to Swansea, on Saturday, 4th March 1961. This was a Bath Road turn for a relatively high-mileage engine, so the crew were fortunate to have an ex-works 'Castle' on the day. The engine was transferred to Old Oak in December 1953, and stayed there until withdrawal in 1962. This cross-country train was subject to a number of engine changes en route, and these arrangements altered over the years. During the summer programme of the mid-1950s, Penzance and Bath Road 'Castles' had shared the duties between those two points; a Canton 'Hall' took the train to Cardiff, and a Landore 'Hall' to Swansea. In the winter 1959/60 rosters, a Penzance engine took the train to Plymouth, a Laira engine on to Bristol, a Bath Road loco to Cardiff and a Canton engine to Swansea. This train arrived at Swansea at 5.15 pm., a 292-mile journey in 9 hours 20 minutes, hardly an 'express' journey. A restaurant car was provided on this service from Plymouth.

Canton 'Castle' No.4073 *Caerphilly Castle* leaving High Street station with the 3.45 p.m. Paddington to Fishguard Harbour on 30th May 1959, with an LNER-design Brake Composite from the Scottish Region (SC10166E) behind the tender. Apart from short allocations to Canton and Landore in 1934/5, *Caerphilly Castle* was an Old Oak engine from 1923 until July 1950, when she went to Bath Road. No.4073 was subsequently transferred to Canton in February 1957 to help out, given the low availability of 'Britannias' transferred there during the previous month, January. Her last major overhaul in traffic was at Swindon in September 1958, and she was taken out of traffic on 10th May 1960 for preservation at the Science Museum, Kensington.

Against a backdrop of the Stow Hill area of Newport, 'Castle' No.5008 *Raglan Castle* is seen easing alongside No.4/5 platform with the 7.30 a.m. Pembroke Dock to Paddington (train A53) on Saturday, 24th September 1960. Leaving Cardiff at 11.48 a.m., this train was the relief to the following 8.0 a.m Neyland (12 noon Cardiff), in whose formation the Pembroke through coaches were normally marshalled; when traffic was heavy, as on summer Saturdays, the Pembroke portion was regularly strengthened to form a relief to the main train. On occasions, this train also started from Cardiff. Built in 1927, No.5008 spent much of her time at Old Oak, firstly from 1933 to 1949, and again from November 1956 until withdrawal in 1962. At this time, Old Oak shed worked the 12.45, 7.55, 11.55 am., 6.55 and 8.55 p.m. departures from Paddington as far as Cardiff or Swansea, returning with the 8.15 a.m. Cardiff, 9.35 p.m., 12.49 a.m., 1.30 and 2.30 p.m. Swansea trains respectively. Again, an ex-LNE coach led the formation for strengthening purposes.

Old Oak 'Castle' No.7024 *Powis Castle* leaving High Street station at the head of the 3.55 p.m. Paddington to Fishguard Harbour (Train 171) in place of the regular Landore 'Castle' (Landore 2 turn) on Thursday, 20th June 1957. No.7024 had probably taken the train over at Paddington in a hurry; this was the 'Capitals United' service, though no headboard was being carried by the engine. An Old Oak engine from new in 1949, No.7024 held the accolade of hauling the last down steam-hauled 'Bristolian on 12th June 1959.

'Austerity' No.90125 from Canton shed approaching Newport station with the class 'F' 4.20 p.m. Ely Paper Mills to Woodford (ER) on Saturday, 30th May 1959. Canton shed ran two eastbound services to Banbury and Woodford using 'Austerities' each afternoon, with two late-evening return trips from the ex-Great Central yards. The signal gantries seen in the background at the eastern portals controlled the routeing options on the two up lines on emerging from the tunnels, including Main to Platform or Through roads.

Another view of the same train moving steadily along the up main road. The 'Austerity' design originated in 1943, with Robin Riddles' work for the then Ministry of Supply. To the left are the gantry signals for the down platform and main roads, placed on the island platform, on the outside of the curve, for better sighting.

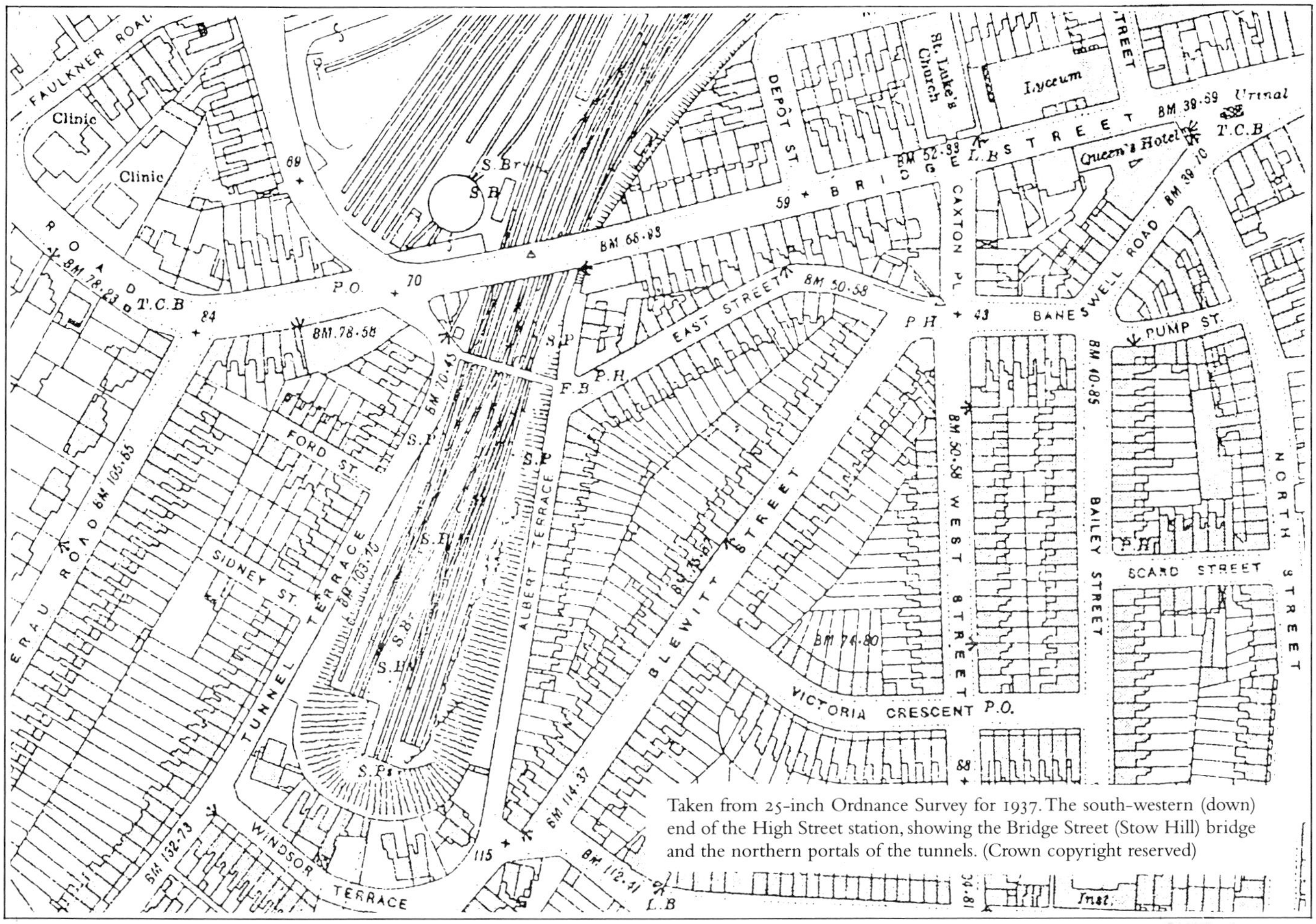

Taken from 25-inch Ordnance Survey for 1937. The south-western (down) end of the High Street station, showing the Bridge Street (Stow Hill) bridge and the northern portals of the tunnels. (Crown copyright reserved)

Ebbw Jct. '28XX' No.2845 trundling out of High Street station with a train of empty mineral wagons on 18th September 1957. Ahead, the two portals of High Street tunnel beckon, with the original bore (main lines) on the left and the 'new' 1910 tunnel (Relief lines) on the right, with the train signalled through the former.

Ebbw Jct. 'Grange' 4–6–0 No.6838 *Goodmoor Grange* accelerating away from High Street and under the roadbridge with a class '6' ('E') mixed freight. The train was signalled across onto the Down Main line from the Down Platform line, and may have been bound for AD Junction given that the first three vehicles were a Conflat with a small container followed by a 'shock' open and a gunpowder van.

No.5066 *Wardour Castle* running along the Up Main with the 3.50 p.m. Whitland to Kensington milk on Thursday, 29th July 1954, with at least two ro-rail tankers in the formation. This engine was renamed *Sir Felix Pole* in April 1956, in honour of the greatest General Manager the GWR ever had. No.5066 went new to Old Oak in 1937, and remained there for the whole of its working life. The Welsh milk and empties trains were worked variously by Old Oak, Swindon, Canton, Landore and Carmarthen engines, with Westbury and Neyland engines also involved at times.

Newport West, with Landore 'Castle' No.5051 *Earl Bathurst* (formerly *Drysllwyn Castle*) seen in pristine condition on the up 'Pembroke Coast Express', 1.5 p.m. Pembroke Dock to Paddington in the summer of 1958. This train was named in 1953 (retained into the '60s), being formed of chocolate-and-cream stock. On its way to London, it called at branch stations to Whitland, then Carmarthen, Llanelly, Swansea, Cardiff and Newport, with a 2½ hour non-stop run for the 133½ miles to Paddington; this timing was similar to those of Welsh expresses of 1914 and 1938. No.5051 was a Landore engine from new in May 1936, and remained there until the shed was closed for dieselisation in 1961, when she moved to Neath.

The evening service saw a trio of immaculate Landore 'Castles' at hourly intervals en route from Swansea to Paddington, leaving Newport at 5.20, 6.20 and 7.20 p.m. The second of these was the up 'South Wales Pullman' (4.30 p.m. Swansea), seen here at Newport West on 9th May 1961 behind Landore 'Castle' No.5062 *Earl of Shaftesbury*. The engine – a late arrival to Landore's stud, moving from Bath Road in September 1960 – was by this time paired with a Hawksworth tender. The Pullman stock worked down to Swansea as the 8.50 a.m. Paddington, and conveyed first and second class passengers. From Newport to Paddington, a supplementary charge of 7s for first class and 4s for second class travel was made on this train in addition to the usual fares (which were 42s and 28s single respectively), with a journey time of 2 hours 25 minutes. The steam-hauled Pullman was replaced by a 'Blue Pullman' train in the summer 1961 programme.

Canton '9F' 2–10–0 No.92003 leaving the gloom of High Street tunnel and passing under Stow Hill road bridge with a class '7' ('F') freight on 9th May 1961. The train comprised empty flat wagons, used in the conveyance of steel plate from Llanwern.

'72XX' 2–8–2T No.7252, from Radyr shed, leaving the Main Line tunnel, probably with the 1.15 p.m. Radyr to Severn Tunnel Jct. coal train during the afternoon of Saturday, 4th March 1961. Other scheduled Radyr '72' duties on mineral trains through Newport around this time included the 1.0 a.m. from Radyr to Severn Tunnel Jct., and the 2.35 a.m. to Salisbury. Work had started on the alterations to the layout, as evidenced by new wooden and chaired sleepers in the foreground, doubtless to be used in the adjustments at the west end of the station.

'County' 4–6–0 No.1022 *County of Northampton* from Shrewsbury shed, running into Newport with the 5.10 p.m. Cardiff to Hereford and Crewe early in 1961. A West Country engine from December 1946, No.1022 moved to Chester in 1951 and thence to Shrewsbury 1958, from where she was withdrawn in 1962. Although most of the class were stationed for use on West Country and Northern trains during the final years of the Great Western era, three engines were sent to Neyland in October 1948, and usually worked as far east as Cardiff. In addition to the coaching stock, this train carried parcels and brake vans from Cardiff to Liverpool, Manchester and Perth.

On 19th May 1964, a down-trodden 'Hall' No.6958 *Oxburgh Hall*, from Pontypool Road, emerging from the north (station) end of the Hillfield Tunnel at Newport West with an up class '6' ('E') freight. In the 1961 alterations, the Relief and Main line designation changed sides through High Street station and the tunnels, and thus matched up to the old designations beyond Gaer Jct. The wagons on the left were empties from Newport Goods which will be taken by the goods pilot to Alexandra Dock Jct. on the evening trip.

HILLFIELD TUNNELS

When the South Wales Railway were planning their railway through Newport, they were confronted by a spur of high ground to the west of the planned station site; this required tunnelling through in order to gain access to the coastal plain beyond, for the continuation westwards to Cardiff. The tunnel was duly bored some 200ft. below the top surface, lower than the springs that then supplied the town's water, causing some of the wells to run dry. In consequence, water had to be imported at great cost. The civil engineers boring the tunnel received a bonus, however, in that the spoil from the works was used to construct and improve the banks of the River Usk, over which the viaduct to carry the line was being constructed. The finished tunnel was 742 yards in length, and accommodated the up and down lines.

Two significant events were to affect the tunnel during the next 30 years. Firstly, the broad gauge tracks were converted to standard gauge in 1872. Then, in 1880, there was a marked increase in traffic, due to the opening by the GWR of a new link line from Park Jct., through a new Gaer Tunnel, to High Street station. This involved the closure to passenger traffic of the previous Dock Street station.

The increase in local passenger traffic was accompanied by a heavy increase in goods (especially coal) traffic, and during the first decade of the new century, it became apparent that a second tunnel was urgently required. Fortunately, this new bore could be made parallel with the original tunnel, on its north side. The work was carried out during 1910/11, and enabled the lines through it to be aligned with those to the Gaer Tunnel branch. Trains to and from the Valleys could use either tunnel, though it seems more likely that they were concentrated on the new tunnel in order to leave the original bore to main-line traffic. At the country end of the tunnels, a new box named Gaer Jct. was created to control the junction of the main line with the Western Valley line, though it is probable that the trains were mostly kept apart. They certainly were after 1928, when the use of the down bay for departing Valley services was discontinued, and Valley trains arrived at and departed from the north face of the island platform.

Heavy retaining walls were built at the High Street end of the new tunnel to support the bank on which there was a housing development, and when the new tunnel was opened, Newport Tunnel box was renamed Newport West. The designation of lines through the tunnels was Mains through the old tunnel and Reliefs through the new.

With the 1961/2 redevelopment of the Newport layout, the designation of lines through the tunnels was reversed. The withdrawal of the local passenger services to the Western Valleys in 1962 considerably increased capacity through the new tunnel, while the old tunnel fed directly into the goods lines which would be used for the new flow of iron ore from Newport Docks to Llanwern, the root cause of the redevelopment. Thus, the lines through the new tunnel now became the Mains and those through the old tunnel the Reliefs; main-line passenger services therefore switched tunnels into and out of High Street station.

FROM GAER JUNCTION TO EBBW JUNCTION

The South Wales main line emerged from Hillfield tunnels on a curve towards the south, and in the following mile passed several important sites and facilities. The provision of the new bore at Hillfield in 1912 and the quadrupling of the line southwards from High Street to Ebbw Jct. to meet up with the 1898/9 four-track development from Cardiff to Ebbw Jct. considerably relieved this bottleneck.

GAER JUNCTION

This junction was located at the south ends of the tunnels, and was the point at which the Gaer branch diverged south-westwards towards Park Jct. for the Western Valleys and Brecon lines, and the major marshalling yard at Rogerstone.

Until 1912 Gaer Jct. box controlled only the double-track junction between the SWML and the Western Valley line. When the new tunnel was built and the lines quadrupled, a double scissors crossover was provided at the tunnel mouths to create maximum flexibility, so that trains emerging from the old tunnel could cross to the Western Valley line (and vice versa), and trains leaving the new tunnel could cross to the new goods lines. The designation of lines through the tunnels and the double scissors was Main Lines through the old tunnel and Relief Lines through the new. General practice was to route Western Valley traffic through the new tunnel and main-line traffic through the old. However, just beyond Gaer Jct. box, the main lines changed over from the east to the west side of the pairs, and passenger traffic to or from Cardiff was provided with higher-speed

Gaer Junction was located at the south end of the High Street tunnels, with crossovers between the Cardiff route lines, and the junction for the Gaer branch to Park Jct. for the valley routes to the north and west. Here Canton '9F' 2–10–0 No.92227 was heading the 2.35 p.m. Cardiff Pengam to Saltney freight towards the old ('Main' line, soon to be 'Relief') tunnel on 2nd March 1961. Included in the train were a 'shockvan' (with vertical white lines) and a cement van. The two crossovers between the Main and Relief lines were of a 'double scissors' design until 1950, when the formation was altered to a simple double junction, as seen here.

The 1.50 p.m. Paddington to Carmarthen emerging from the original tunnel behind Westbury 'Hall' No.4930 *Hagley Hall* on 30th July1957. The train number '168' was in use for the 1.50 pm. Paddington from 1952 until 1957, having previously been '944'; in summer 1958, it became '171', '724' in summer 1959, and '(1)F44' in the four-digit scheme of summer 1960. The remains of the disconnected part of the 'double scissors junction' may be seen alongside the front coaches of the train.

crossovers for this purpose. Cardiff goods services simply carried on ahead, down the goods road.

In 1950, the section of the double scissors crossover at the mouth of the tunnels from the relief lines (new tunnel) to the main lines (old tunnel) was taken out, presumably through lack of use, freight trains to and from the goods lines beyond Gaer Jct. being routed through the old tunnel, with the facility remaining to route Rogerstone-bound freights from the old tunnel across to the Western Valley line.

Under the alterations to layout in 1961, additional single crossovers were provided to create maximum flexibility under reversible working, and the designation of lines through the tunnels was reversed, the main lines now merging with the Western Valley route and passing through the new tunnel and the relief lines through the old tunnel. The level of track occupation determined which route would be taken by passenger services into and out of High Street station. With the introduction of reversible working arrangements in November 1961, Gaer Jct. box was taken out of use, and a temporary control panel installed in the box's interlocking relay room until December 1962, when the functions of the temporary panels were transferred to the new Panel Box at High Street.

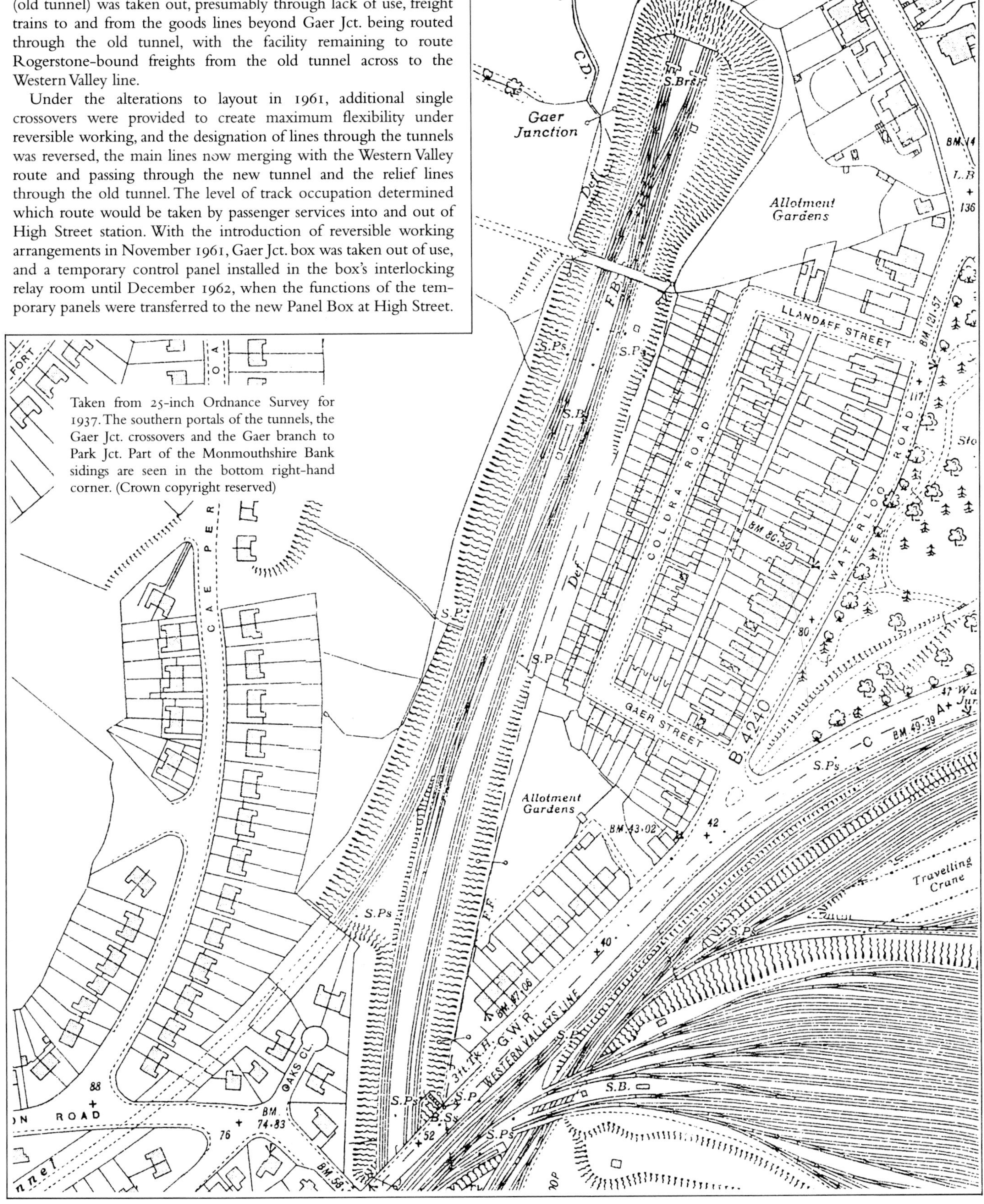

Taken from 25-inch Ordnance Survey for 1937. The southern portals of the tunnels, the Gaer Jct. crossovers and the Gaer branch to Park Jct. Part of the Monmouthshire Bank sidings are seen in the bottom right-hand corner. (Crown copyright reserved)

It was always a rewarding experience when two trains could be photographed together. This view taken on 2nd March 1961, shows an '87XX' 0–6–0PT heading a Western Valleys train for Newport into the up 'Relief' line ('new') tunnel, and No.6941 *Fillongley Hall* from Gloucester shed on the Up Main at the head of the 8.48 a.m. Fishguard to Paddington parcels. The parcels train spent around ten minutes at High Street station, and was then routed via Gloucester and Swindon, it conveyed vehicles from a number of South Wales locations to Gloucester, Wolverhampton, Nottingham, Swindon, Kensington and, for the majority of the vans, Paddington. The main (Paddington) part of this train comprised returning empty newspaper and other vans off the 12.45 a.m. Paddington to Carmarthen.

'42XX' 2–8–0T No.5258 drifting towards the new tunnel with a coal train from the Western Valleys line via Park Jct. and the Gaer branch, on 2nd March 1961. The original No.5258 (of 1926) was converted into '72XX' class 2–8–2T No.7223 in 1935; the replacement seen here was built in February 1940, and allocated to Aberdare. In 1961, the engine was still at Aberdare, and may therefore have been working through on one of the turns to Severn Tunnel Jct.

Banbury 'Austerity' 2–8–0 No.90148 heading towards the new tunnel with an up mixed freight from Rogerstone on the evening of Thursday, 2nd March 1961. The first two containers, marked for the carriage of biscuits from Huntley & Palmers, were probably returning to Reading. This area is now overgrown with trees, making an open view photograph such as this impossible.

Ebbw Jct. '28XX' No.3827 getting away from the old tunnel with a down class '6' ('E') fast freight on 2nd March 1961. As the gantries were so close to the portals, the down signals had been placed to coincide with the apex of the tunnel bore, and were low enough to permit sighting by engine crews still in the tunnel.

St. Philip's Marsh 'County' 4–6–0 No.1027 *County of Stafford* leaving High Street main-line tunnel with train 'F38' – the 7.55 am. Penzance to Swansea, on Thursday, 2nd March 1961. No.1027 had been at Neyland from November 1950, but was transferred to Bath Road in October 1959, and to St. Philip's Marsh in September 1960. The engine was withdrawn from traffic at Shrewsbury in September 1963, and condemned soon afterwards at Swindon. This duty had previously been part of a Shrewsbury turn, running the Penzance train from Bristol to Cardiff, then continuing with the 9.48 p.m. parcels from Cardiff to Crewe as far as Shrewsbury.

No.7202, from Radyr shed, returning from Severn Tunnel Jct. with a class '8' ('H') freight on 2nd March 1961, with some empty bogie flat steel carriers for Guest, Keens at Cardiff in the train. With the overall decline in coal traffic conveyed, the metal industries assumed an added importance for revenue. It was unusual to see these engines working bunker first on the main line; perhaps on this occasion, the crew wanted to get home with a minimum of delay.

The continual South Wales cycle is illustrated in this view, with '72XX' No.7203 (from Aberdare) emerging from the new tunnel with a train of down mineral empties, whilst a loaded train of coal was making its way northwards into the old tunnel. The '72' would shortly swing off the Relief line to take the Gaer Loop branch to Park Jct. and the Western Valley route home. When private owner wagons for coal traffic were taken over by the government during the Second World War, the fleet was 'pooled', and this led to mineral empties being called 'pools', a name which stuck for as long as the traffic survived.

'9F' 2–10–0 No.92002 (Ebbw Jct.) running off the Gaer branch from Park Jct. with a class 'H' train, largely of mineral traffic from Rogerstone on 2nd March 1961. The '9Fs' were particularly found on Banbury and Woodford trains from Rogerstone. The main-line layout to the south of Gaer Jct. can be seen in this view, as can Gaer Jct. signal box (which would close in November of that year) behind the first wagon on the train.

A photograph that could only be taken from a passing train, in this instance the 11.10 a.m. Swansea to Penzance on 10th May 1958. Having emerged from Gaer tunnel, '42XX' 2–8–0T No.5263 (from Aberdare shed) is seen running down the gradient towards Gaer Jct. with a train of coal, probably for Severn Tunnel Jct. In addition to the various freight services from Aberdare, Rogerstone and Bassaleg yards, passenger trains on the Caerphilly, Brecon and Brynmawr routes also used this line. The 403-yard Gaer tunnel can be seen in the background, burrowing under the outskirts of that suburb to connect lines from the valleys to the main lines for Newport and the east.

A very dirty Carmarthen 'Castle', No.7009 *Athelney Castle*, accelerating away from Gaer Jct with the 9.20 a.m. Manchester (London Road) to Swansea ('V54') service on 2nd March 1961. The engine visited Swindon the following month for a 'Heavy General' overhaul, which took about two months to complete. In the four-character identification system introduced in summer 1960, trains originating from outside the Western Region used the letter 'V', whilst those running to other regions used 'M' (LMR), 'E' (ER), 'N' (NER), 'O' (SR) or 'S' (ScR). Gaer Jct. signal box, seen in the background near the tunnels, was closed in November 1961, though a temporary panel was operative inside for a year afterwards.

A panoramic view of the Gaer Jct area looking north, taken after the installation of the MAS system, with the junction's box removed. Having passed westwards over the Usk viaduct, the main line then took up a gradual left-hand curve around to the south, passing through High Street station and tunnels on the way. In this view, the Gaer branch can be seen descending towards the main route from the left, whilst the main lines descend southwards at 1 in 100 towards the level section through Alexandra Dock and Ebbw Junctions on the south-western outskirts of the town. Worcester (former Llanelly) 'Castle' No.5054 *Earl of Ducie* is seen accelerating away down the gradient with a Derbyshire Railway Society special on the Down Relief line during 1964.

Canton '9F' No.92220 *Evening Star* leaving Gaer Jct. with the down 'Capitals United', the 3.55 p.m. from Paddington to Fishguard Harbour, on 28th June 1960. The train was about to cross under the A48 road bridge, which carries the main Cardiff and Carmarthen road out of Newport. Immediately to the south of the road-bridge, the line from Dock Street to Park Jct. and the valleys also crossed over the main line, and just beyond that was Alexandra Dock Jct. and its yards on the east (down) side of the line. On the southern outskirts of the town, some three-quarters of a mile from Gaer Jct, was the large engine shed at Ebbw Junction.

ALEXANDRA DOCK JUNCTION, MAESGLAS & ROGERSTONE YARDS

During the last years of the 19th century, in addition to the quadrupling of the running lines between Cardiff and Alexandra Dock Jct. ('AD Jct.' to the locals), completed in 1898, improved marshalling facilities were provided there, expanding on the previous access lines to and from the Docks. By 1900, there were eight mostly double-ended sidings, two with long shunting spurs at the west end, opposite Ebbw Jct. Signal Box. East of the access into these sidings, another small nest of four double-ended sidings was provided between the main access lines to and from the Docks, opposite the new Alexandra Dock Jct. Signal Box, opened in 1899. To cater for traffic in the First World War, a further twelve sidings, stop-blocked at the west end, were installed, given the name Field Sidings, and in 1925/6, fifteen sidings known as Eastern Valley Sidings plus two through running roads, were laid in, curving hard round from Waterloo Loop Signal Box back towards the Docks. Seven Low Level Loop Sidings were also laid in and in the space between these and EV Sdgs., another nest of six sidings, called New Sidings, was added with the same curving configuration.

The dock lines centred around two main banks of sidings on the east (docks) side of the main line. At the northern end was the Monmouthshire Bank (or 'Mon Bank'), a huge raft of some 45 sidings split between down and up, which funnelled at the west end through Maesglas Jct. and curved out at the south end through East Mendalgief Jct. ('East Men'). To the south of these was the Mendalgief Bank, again of about 45 sidings split fairly evenly between down and up and which funnelled at the west end past West Mendalgief Signal Box ('West Men') and radiated at the south end from East Mendalgief box, which stood outside Pill engine shed.

Pill shed, which took over from Dock Street in 1929, provided the power for dock shunting and tripping and local mineral working in the form of '42XXs', saddle and pannier tanks, and constituent engines. In later years, motive power was largely '42XXs' and '67XXs', the shed closing in 1963.

Park Jct. was the point at which three routes converged to enter the Western Valley route, and was located about a half-mile to the west of the SWML. The original line from the Western Valleys ran straight into Maesglas yard, the extension of which to Courtybella Jct. and the docks crossed the SWML a half-mile to the south of Gaer Jct. Park Jct. itself was formed when the Gaer branch connected with that line.

The third route from Park Jct. comprised the two running lines to West Mendalgief box, which crossed the main line by means of a very substantial black panelled bridge just to the north of Ebbw Jct., first installed in 1885. This route, taken by the Newport Docks to Ebbw Vale iron ore traffic, was closed in 1959, possibly due to the condition of the bridge, which was a feature of the main line at that point, and the traffic routed through Mon Bank and Maesglas Jct. to Park Jct. This nullified the use of Mendalgief Bank, and the sidings were recovered between 1966–67. Between 1977–79, almost the whole of Mon Bank was recovered, little further proof being required of the level of reduction of freight traffic in the area.

Alexandra Dock Jct. Yard was the main marshalling yard for Newport, and was always very busy. It was a difficult yard to work due to cramped working conditions, and was essentially on two levels with Maesglas Yard, which had previously served the docks before the opening of Mon and Mendalgief Banks. AD Jct's problems were accentuated by a badly-planned closure of Pontypool Road Yard in 1965, following the closure of the Vale of Neath as a through route, and the level of traffic throughput often reached saturation point with the yard on stop until traffic could be sorted and cleared.

AD Jct. was not a coal traffic yard, other than for local mileage yards and small industrial concerns. Coal traffic from the Western Valley pits was marshalled at Rogerstone Yard at the south end of the Western Valleys line, and then went forward via Bassaleg and Park Jct. to the main line, eastwards via the Gaer Tunnel and Gaer Jct. and westwards via the Cardiff Curve and Ebbw Jct. Rogerstone Yard was open by 1885, when it consisted of seven down side loop sidings with three further stop-blocked and appropriate shunting necks, with a similar (though not identical) layout on the up side. In 1900, the main Western Valley running lines were diverted away from passing through the centre of the yard to run behind the down yard, and six relief lines were created (from the previous two mains and two reliefs) presumably to enable trains to attach and detach without actually entering the yard itself. The yard was extended in 1931, the down side becoming a Hump Yard with 16 loop sidings coming off the hump, while the up side yard was extended to 29 sidings, of which 19 were stop-blocked at the south end. The yard played an important role in marshalling trains for mainline destinations, including trains of loco coal for principal GWR depots and SR depots in the south-west. With the cessation of this traffic in the early 1960s, the NCB used the coal in a blended and treated form to supply Llanwern and Margam steelworks as prime coking coal. An appraisal of all South Wales coal traffic during 1968 found that 95% of coal produced in the Western Valley could be worked in block trains through from pit to destination, and Rogerstone Down Side Yard was therefore closed, the up side being retained as an empty mineral wagon holding yard. Residual traffic from Rogerstone Yard was handled at Severn Tunnel Jct. Yard. As the volume of South Wales coal declined, the supply of empty mineral wagons for the Western Valley was undertaken from East Usk, and by 1977 Rogerstone Up Side yard was recovered.

Goods trains from AD Jct. and Rogerstone were destined for all parts of the system (and beyond), with fast services to Paddington, Bristol, Newton Abbot, Hockley and Saltney, amongst others. To the east and south, heavier services ran to and from Old Oak, Acton, Hanwell Bridge, Reading, Bristol, Hackney, Laira, Salisbury and Gloucester. There were many trains to and from yards in the Midlands and the North, including Banbury, Leamington, Worcester, Yarnton, Stourbridge Jct., Bordesley Jct., Oxley, Coton Hill and Saltney. Numerous services ran locally, with many to and from Severn Tunnel Jct.

Alexandra Dock Jct. Yard remains in use alongside the main line, with traffic levels a mere fraction of their previous level, and Enterprise trains (the modern equivalent of wagonload services) use the yard, often with the most modest of loads. AD Jct. is the only main yard left in the area since the demise of Severn Tunnel Jct., and now copes easily with what should have been its role throughout as the main line yard for Newport.

WATERLOO LOOP

Waterloo Loop included the area of track that climbed from the north of AD Jct. yard to the high level at Maesglas, which was joined at Waterloo Jct. box. Originally, access to the line at the low-level end was via a ground frame worked in association with the high-level box, but probably when facilities were improved in the area during 1898/99, Waterloo Loop box was opened at the low level, though no exact date has been found. The high-level box was closed in 1923 and a new box provided at the low level in 1926. This in turn was closed during the alterations to layout of 1961 and a new box provided, largely independent of Newport Panel, as most movements controlled were over local freight lines and yard connections with no direct bearing on the main line. However, certain crossovers between the relief lines and the freight lines controlled by Waterloo Loop are operated from Newport Panel.

As the Waterloo Loop line climbed around north-eastwards from the low to the high level, it passed under the line from Maesglas Jct. into Mon Bank, the route originally taken by trains of shipment coal from the Western and Sirhowy Valleys into the docks. When the bridge carrying the line from West Mendalgief to Park Jct. was closed in 1959, the iron ore services from Newport Docks to Ebbw Vale were diverted to run this way. The high-level line from Maesglas past the former Waterloo Jct. box, was part of the original line to Newport from the Western Valley and ran on past the site of the first passenger station in Newport at Courtybella, alongside the A48 road from Newport to Cardiff. It is hoped to discuss this, and the numerous other valleys and docks lines in a further volume.

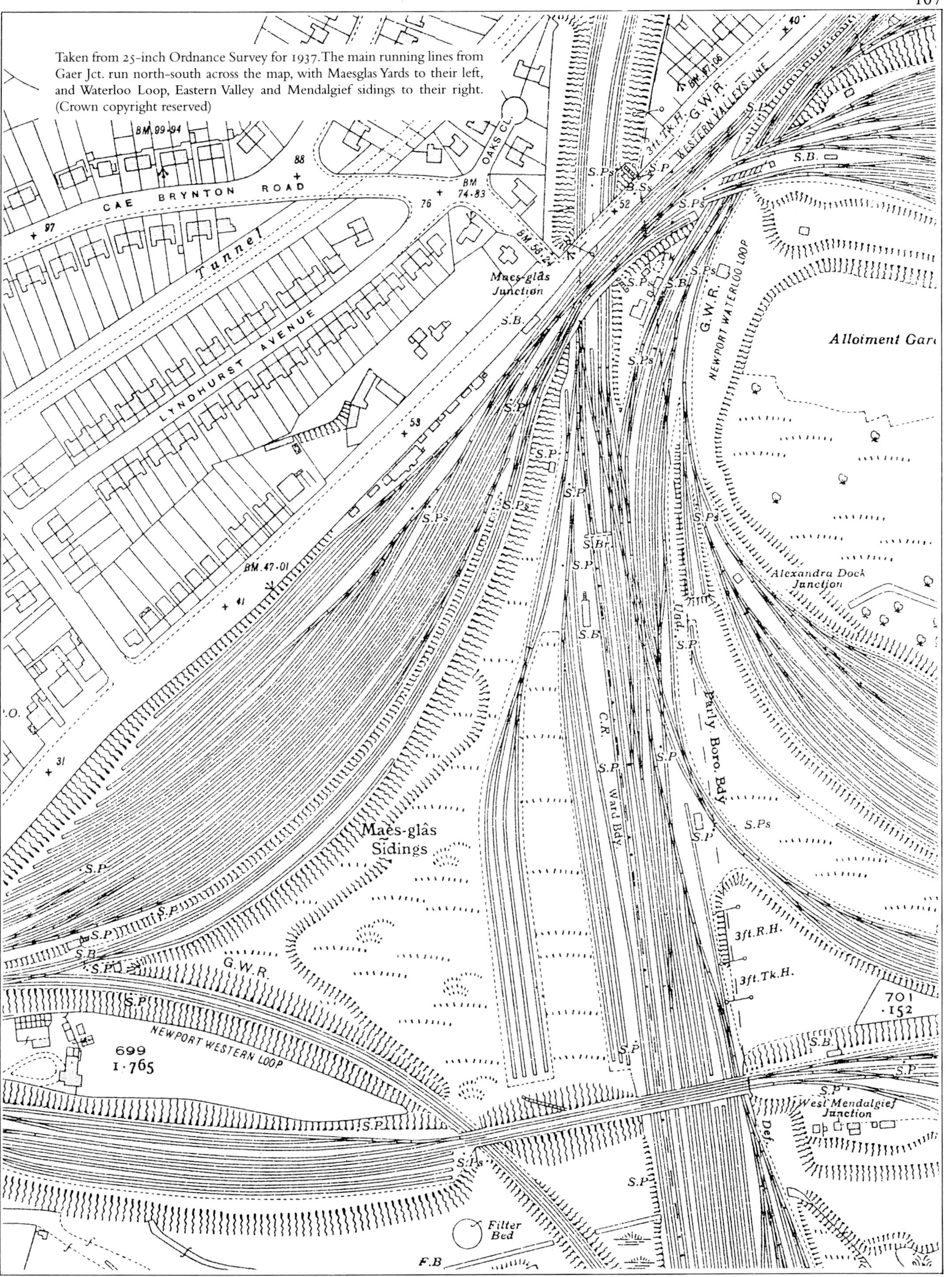

Taken from 25-inch Ordnance Survey for 1937. The main running lines from Gaer Jct. run north-south across the map, with Maesglas Yards to their left, and Waterloo Loop, Eastern Valley and Mendalgief sidings to their right. (Crown copyright reserved)

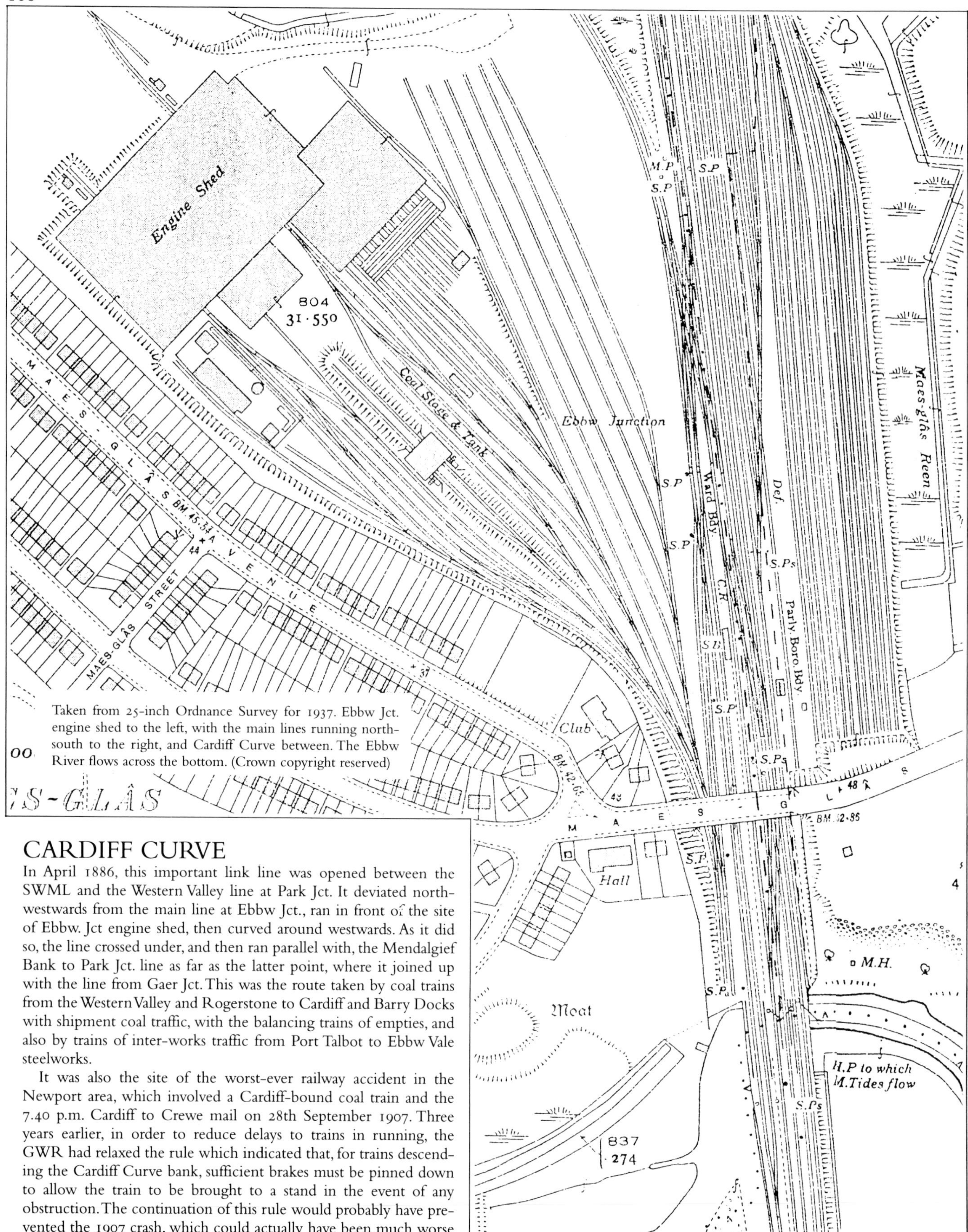

Taken from 25-inch Ordnance Survey for 1937. Ebbw Jct. engine shed to the left, with the main lines running north-south to the right, and Cardiff Curve between. The Ebbw River flows across the bottom. (Crown copyright reserved)

CARDIFF CURVE

In April 1886, this important link line was opened between the SWML and the Western Valley line at Park Jct. It deviated north-westwards from the main line at Ebbw Jct., ran in front of the site of Ebbw. Jct engine shed, then curved around westwards. As it did so, the line crossed under, and then ran parallel with, the Mendalgief Bank to Park Jct. line as far as the latter point, where it joined up with the line from Gaer Jct. This was the route taken by coal trains from the Western Valley and Rogerstone to Cardiff and Barry Docks with shipment coal traffic, with the balancing trains of empties, and also by trains of inter-works traffic from Port Talbot to Ebbw Vale steelworks.

It was also the site of the worst-ever railway accident in the Newport area, which involved a Cardiff-bound coal train and the 7.40 p.m. Cardiff to Crewe mail on 28th September 1907. Three years earlier, in order to reduce delays to trains in running, the GWR had relaxed the rule which indicated that, for trains descending the Cardiff Curve bank, sufficient brakes must be pinned down to allow the train to be brought to a stand in the event of any obstruction. The continuation of this rule would probably have prevented the 1907 crash, which could actually have been much worse as the down main-line signals at Ebbw Jct. had also been cleared for the down Irish Boat train, which fortunately was brought to a stand in time.

EBBW JUNCTION ENGINE SHED

With the increase in the number of engines required to handle the vast amounts of coal being produced in the Monmouthshire pits in the early years of the 20th century, much of which was for movement to Newport Docks, it became necessary to provide a much larger engine shed to cover this and main-line commitments at Newport, too great to be covered by the original SWR depot at High Street. The GWR therefore constructed a large depot on land at Maesglas in 1915, on the opposite side of the line to their Alexandra Dock Jct. Yard. The depot was a standard Churchward two-unit shed, consisting of two large roundhouses and a large repair shop. Each roundhouse unit contained a 65ft turntable of the undergirder type, from which radiated 28 roads between 41 and 100ft. in length, giving total accommodation of some 36 tender and 28 tank engines. Provision was made for further expansion if necessary.

The ash road and coal stage (with 146,000-gallon capacity water tank over) was centrally located between the incoming roads to each roundhouse, the two feed roads either side enabling engines to run forward into the shed. All the usual facilities provided were on a large scale befitting the size and importance of the depot. The stores, shed foremen's offices, and enginemen's messrooms were on the south side of the shed, with messrooms for mechanics, cleaners and

A view of Ebbw Jct. repair shop from the main lines on 22nd September 1962, with the engine shed to its left. The front of the former building housed the lifting shop, with smiths' and other shops behind.

'WDs' Nos.90365 and 90520 at Ebbw Jct shed on 8th July 1951. Both engines were from Woodford Halse (ER) shed, which was linked as much to Western Region goods traffic, via the ex-GC line to Banbury, as it was to its own. That shed's WD engines were to be found on many parts of the Western Region, including Old Oak, Southall, Stoke Gifford, and Gloucester, with three daily block loads (or mixed, when not available) to Severn Tunnel Jct., Rogerstone, Alexandra Dock Jct. or Cardiff. The engines are seen standing outside the westernmost roundhouse of the shed.

Ebbw Jct. was the first depot on BR to receive an allocation of the new Standard class '9Fs' in 1954 for working the Newport Docks to Ebbw Vale steelworks iron ore trains. They languished for some six months on shed, awaiting modifications, before they were able to commence work on those services, when they did, they were used two per train, the second engine banking. These pictures show Nos.92004 and 92003 back-to-back outside the fitting/repair shop at their home shed on 13th March 1954, before the modifications were effected, with a closer view of the 5,000-gallon (BR1G) tender attached to these engines in the second illustration.

The '9Fs' slowly gravitated onto general main-line services, and when the new allocation of double-chimneyed locomotives (922XX series) appeared on the Western Region, some of the earlier engines were fitted with double chimneys and transferred away, replaced by the new batch. In May 1961, there were five of the earlier and twelve of the later engines at Ebbw Jct; by late 1963, there were just eight of the '922XX' series at Ebbw Jct. Here, No.92006 is pictured inside Ebbw Jct. shed on 24th March 1963.

others on the east side, The yard was lit by incandescent gas, and equipped with outside pits and water cranes. A large detached sand furnace was located at the rear of the shed.

On the south-east corner of the depot was a large lifting shop, 197ft x 112ft, containing twelve 52ft pits, with a wood-block floor. An overhead electric crane of 35-ton capacity and 49ft span was provided, running on roads 23ft. above rail level. In front of the shop was an electric traverser, capable of handling the largest locomotives, and also a weighbridge and house with five locomotive balancing tables. Behind the factory were the smith's shop, containing a furnace, steam hammer, and six smith's single and one double hearth. The coppersmith and carpenters had shops alongside. With the onset of the 1914–18 war, part of the new fitting shop was immediately acquired when new by the Ministry of Munitions for use as a shell factory.

When the depot opened, provision needed to be made for the level of movements on and off shed at the main-line junction and a new 91-lever frame was installed in Ebbw Jct. box outside the depot to provide for the additional requirement. Many engine movements to and from the depot were made via the Cardiff Curve, which ran along the front of the depot then curved around the rear. This gave access to Maesglas and Park Jct. and enabled the other side of the main line to be reached if necessary without making conflicting movements across.

In January 1930, the shed housed 20 tender engines of the 'Bulldog', '28XX', '30XX', '26XX', '43XX' and '2301' classes, along with 44 '42XXs', 15 '45XXs', 11 '56XXs' and a '3150'. There were forty of the older 0–6–0 saddle and pannier tanks, with six of the new '57XXs'. Two '517' 0–4–2Ts and a 'Metro' 2–4–0T, with a handful of B&M designs, completed the allocation.

By early 1939, Ebbw Jct. shed contained about 155 engines. Its role continued primarily as a goods engine depot, with 88 such turns shared between its '28XX', '30XX', '43XX', '26XX', '68XX', '72XX', '42XX', '56XX', '57XX' and other tank classes, including ex-Brecon & Merthyr locomotives. The 26 shunting, banking and pilot turns were carried out by the '42XX', '57XX', '1854', '2021', '2721' and constituent engines. Passenger duties amounted to 18, and were worked by the '29XX', '45XX', '2301', '64XX', '48XX', '3150', '57XX' and B&M 0–6–2Ts.

At nationalisation, the shed had twelve 4–6–0s of the 'Hall' (5), 'Grange' (5) and 'Saint' (2) classes, with eighteen '28XXs', two 'Austerities', two '43XXs', one '2301' and three '2251s'. Heavy tank engines included 9 '72XXs', 32 '42XXs', 8 '56XXs' and a '31XX'. Of the other tanks, there were 6 '45XXs', 5 '64XX' and 37 other panniers, a '14XX' 0–4–2T and 4 ex-B&M engines.

As the steam age neared its end, there was still a good variety of engines at Ebbw Jct. In January 1959 the allocation was:

'Grange'	6	'51XX,	2
'Hall'	1	'56XX'	2
'28XX'	18	'64XX'	6
'Austerity'	6	'57XX'	30
'92XXX'	11	'15XX'	1
'43XX'	2	'16XX'	1
'72XX'	14	'2251'	2
'42XX'	26	'94XX'	9
'3100'	1		

Ebbw Jct. shed, with one of its allocation of '42XXs', No.5236, standing at the coal stage on 24th March 1963. The '42s' were the mainstay of coal train working in the Newport Valleys, though they did not begin to replace the large numbers of six-coupled tanks on those duties until the Great War; by January 1918, there were no less than 37 of the engines at Ebbw Jct., out of 61 then in traffic. The number exceeded 60 at the time of Grouping, but gradually decreased to around 35 at Nationalisation with the decline of coal traffic. By 1963, there were about a dozen at Ebbw Jct.

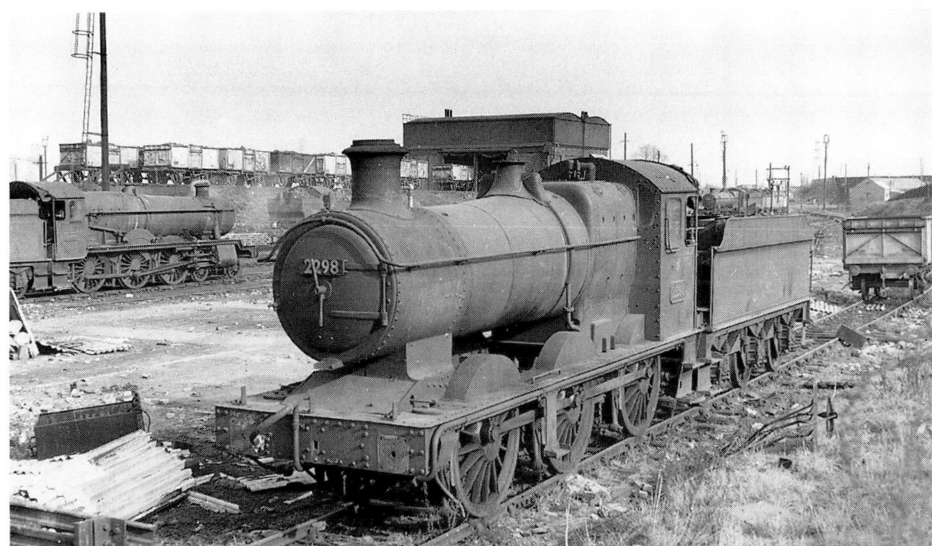

A rather derelict '2251' 0–6–0 No.2298 'in store' on the western sidings at Ebbw Jct. shed on 24th March 1963. This engine had only been at Ebbw Jct. for a short time, having worked on the Cambrian section from new in 1938. The coal stage with water tower over can be seen beyond the engine.

The shed at Ebbw Jct was home to a few constituent engines from the Brecon & Merthyr and Alexandra Docks companies after grouping, though most were still at Pill or Bassaleg. From the 1930s, only ex-Brecon & Merthyr engines were usually at Ebbw Jct. shed, mostly 0–6–2Ts. Here, ex-B & M 0–6–2T No.436 is seen alongside the coal stage at Ebbw Jct. in April 1950; originally B & M No.50, she carried the GWR number 1670 until October 1949, when it was renumbered 436. This engine was withdrawn in February 1954.

Resplendent in a new coat of paint from an overhaul at Caerphilly works, '72XX' 2–8–2T No.7232 at Ebbw Jct. shed on 15th April 1962, parked in the sidings at the southern end of the shed. The engine was built from No.5267 in August 1935, and arrived at Ebbw Jct. in May 1952, moving on to Llanelly in January 1959. By 1963, there were no '72s' left at Ebbw Jct., though other sheds in the Principality still housed them, and visitors were regular. The size of these locomotives is well illustrated in this view – No.7232 was some 4ft longer than the locomotive she was constructed from, with water tanks increased from 1,800 to 2,500 gallons for main-line work. At 92½ tons full, she was some 10 tons heavier than the '42s'.

Canton 'Grange' No.6833 *Calcot Grange* crossing the Ebbw River with the seven-coach 5.43 p.m Cardiff to Gloucester service at Ebbw Jct. on Tuesday, 28th June 1960. Though Canton was one of the first sheds to receive 'Granges', in 1936, the allocation of five was transferred away in the summer of 1948, and it was not until 1959 that another example was moved in. No.6833 became a Canton engine in January 1960, transferred from St. Philip's Marsh; her condition did nothing for Canton's reputation, but in November of that year she went to Swindon factory for a 'Heavy General', and was turned out in the usual pristine condition. The engine was transferred to Penzance in February 1962. In the distance, the line can be seen curving gently around Ebbw carriage shed, which had five internal sidings, with another three to its right, bordering on the river. A short distance to the south of Ebbw Jct., the main line curved around to the south-west, to parallel the coast on its way to Cardiff.

Landore 'Castle' No.7028 *Cadbury Castle* crossing the Ebbw River bridge, near Ebbw Jct. Loco, with 'The South Wales Pullman', 4.30 p.m. from Swansea, on 28th June 1960. This was the last scheduled year of operation under steam power, after which the 'Blue Pullman' took over the working. The two lines in the immediate foreground were the spurs to Ebbw Jct. shed, which was behind the photographer in this view. Though eight months out of shops, the engine still commanded one of Landore's top turns, a tribute to her general condition and to Landore's maintenance.

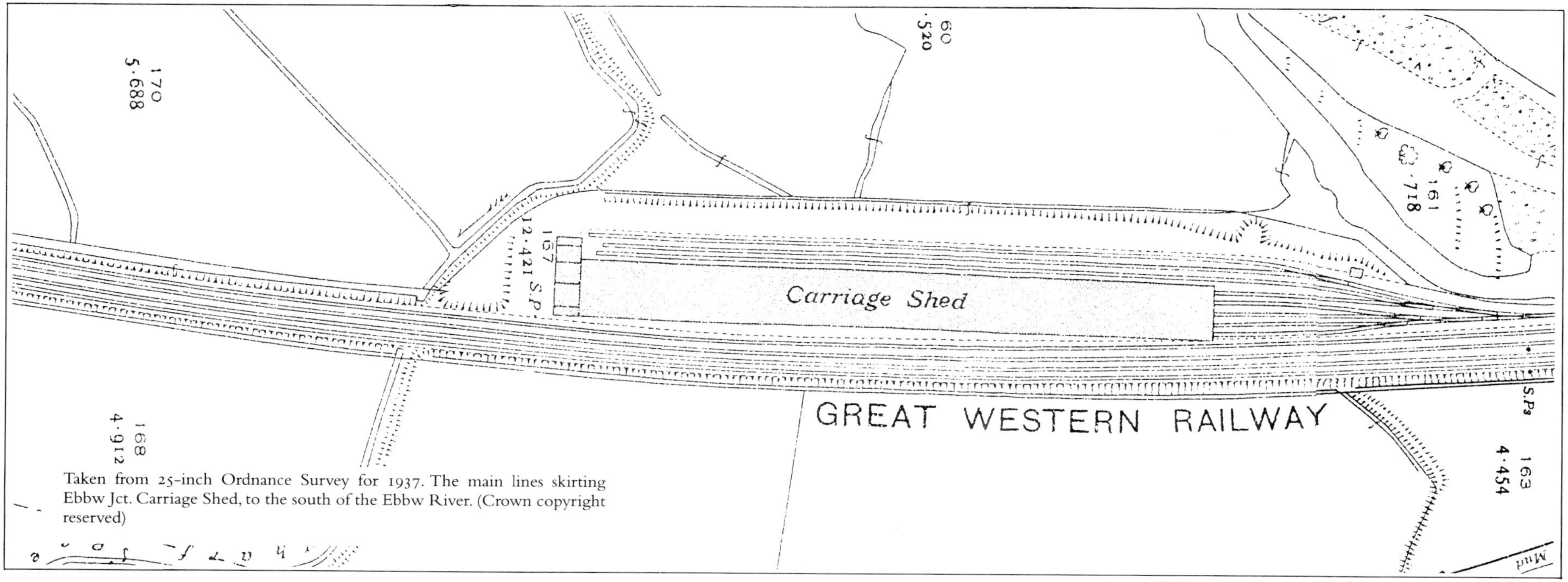

Taken from 25-inch Ordnance Survey for 1937. The main lines skirting Ebbw Jct. Carriage Shed, to the south of the Ebbw River. (Crown copyright reserved)

TRACK REDESIGNATION AND MULTIPLE ASPECT SIGNALLING
(April 1961 to December 1962)

A '42XX' 2–8–0T and 2–8–2T '72XX' No.7212 (from Ebbw Jct. shed) crossing at the west end of Newport station with the usual pattern of down empties and up loaded coal trains on 15th April 1961. The sight and sound of unfitted goods trains rattling through the middle roads of stations like Newport was most distinctive, with the beat of wheels on rail joints and the clatter of buffers when brakes were applied. Sadly, it is now lost to us.

The opening of the Llanwern Steelworks in 1961 required the movement of large tonnages of imported iron ore from Newport Docks by rail, joining the main line at Alexandra Dock Jct. and entering the steelworks at the west end of the complex. In addition, large quantities of coking coal, mainly from the Western Valley collieries, joined the main line at Gaer Jct. From Newport East to Llanwern, the track order at this time was Up Relief, Up Main, Down Main, Down Relief, and the slow-moving iron ore and coal trains, having been crossed to the Up Relief at Newport East or Maindee, would have had to cross back over both the Up and Down Mains and the Down Relief at Llanwern to enter the works, an untenable situation which would have caused heavy delays to main-line traffic.

The answer lay in redesignating the tracks so that between AD Jct. and Llanwern, the relief lines ran on the south side, and the order became (from the North) Up Main, Down Main, Up Relief, Down Relief; the relief lines were thus located on the coastal side through from Cardiff Newtown. As the signalling was largely of 1928 vintage, the opportunity was taken to update the area with latest state-of-the-art Multiple Aspect Signalling, controlled from one panel box located at High Street. At the east end of the Llanwern complex, a flyover was built for eastward-bound 'finished' traffic and home iron ore empties to gain access to the up side at Severn Tunnel Junction yard.

In April 1961, the first stage of reconstruction included the redesignation of tracks, new connections into and out of Llanwern, and construction of the new single-track flyover at Bishton. Temporary local control panels were brought into use at East Usk and Maindee Main to allow the existing boxes at Llanwern, Lliswerry Crossing, East Usk Jct. and Maindee Jct. East to be closed, and Bishton to be converted to a ground frame to cover the level crossing.

The next stage provided automatic signalling on the North & West main line between Maindee North Jct. and Llantarnam, with the closure of Caerleon and Ponthir boxes. This was followed in November 1961 by the introduction of further reversible working at Newport High Street, and automatic signalling to the west of Hillfield Tunnels between Gaer Jct. and AD Jct. A temporary control panel was set up in the Gaer Jct. interlocking relay room, and a new mechanical box was opened at Waterloo Loop, enabling the existing boxes at Gaer Jct., Alexandra Dock Jct., Waterloo Loop and Maesglas Sidings (on the HL line) to be closed.

Further modifications again involved the North & West line with the completion of the resignalling between Maindee and Llantarnam, already started, and the SWML area at Maindee with a temporary control panel installed in the relay room at Maindee North box.

The most important stage took place in December 1962, by which time trains were fully operational over the new layout at High Street, the Valley passenger service having been withdrawn the previous April. This involved the transfer of the functions of the four temporary panels and the Newport East and West boxes into the new central panel box, located at the east end of the former down platform. The final stage, achieved in 1963, was the conversion to colour light signalling under the control of Newport Panel between Ebbw Jct. and St. Brides (the boundary between the Newport and Cardiff Districts), and closure of the boxes. The coverage of the Newport Panel was finally extended to include the Magor-Severn Tunnel in 1968/9, involving the closure of Magor, Severn Tunnel Junction West, Middle and East and Severn Tunnel West boxes.

All photographs by John Hodge with the exception of the following: R. O. Tuck – p. 8 (lower), p. 36 (top & middle), p. 42, p. 43 (top & bottom), p. 50, p. 51, p. 80, p. 86, p. 87 (top & bottom), p. 94 (middle), p. 110 (top & bottom). F. K. Davies – p. 13, p. 15 (top & bottom), p. 17 (top), p. 70, p. 111, p. 112, p. 113 (top & middle). Collection R. S. Carpenter – p. 14, p. 109 (top). S. Rickard, cty. Brian Miller – p. 31 (top), p. 36 (bottom), p. 37, p. 38, p. 41 (top & bottom). Hugh Davies – p. 46, p. 49. W. Potter, cty. Kidderminster Railway Museum – p. 12. Brian Moone, cty. Kidderminster Railway Museum – p. 17 (bottom). G. Sanders, cty. Kidderminster Railway Museum – p. 109 (bottom). Celyn Leigh Jones – p. 113 (bottom).

SOURCES: R. A. Cooke: *Track Layout Diagrams of the GWR: Newport*; Herbert Williams: *Railways in Wales.*